PRESERVES

PRESERVES

140 DELICIOUS JAMS, JELLIES AND RELISHES SHOWN IN 220 PHOTOGRAPHS

CATHERINE ATKINSON & MAGGIE MAYHEW

southwater

This edition is published by Southwater,
an imprint of Anness Publishing Ltd, Blaby Road,
Wigston, Leicestershire LE18 4SE; info@anness.com

www.southwaterbooks.com; www.annesspublishing.com

If you like the images in this book and would like to
investigate using them for publishing, promotions or
advertising, please visit www.practicalpictures.com
for more information.

A CIP catalogue record for this book is available from
the British Library.

Publisher: Joanna Lorenz
Senior Managing Editor: Conor Kilgallon
Editor: Amy Christian
Recipes: Catherine Atkinson and Maggie Mayhew
Photography: Craig Robertson
Stylist: Helen Trent
Home Economist: Sarah O'Brien
Designed by the Bridgewater Book Company Ltd
Production Controller: Don Campaniello

NOTES

Bracketed terms are intended for American readers.
For all recipes, quantities are given in both metric and
imperial measures and, where appropriate, in standard
cups and spoons. Follow one set of measures, but not
a mixture, because they are not interchangeable.
Standard spoon and cup measures are level. 1 tsp = 5ml,
1 tbsp = 15ml, 1 cup = 250ml/8fl oz.
Australian standard tablespoons are 20ml. Australian
readers should use 3 tsp in place of 1 tbsp for measuring
small quantities.
American pints are 16fl oz/2 cups. American readers
should use 20fl oz/2.5 cups in place of 1 pint when
measuring liquids.
Electric oven temperatures in this book are for
conventional ovens. When using a fan oven, the
temperature will probably need to be reduced by about
10–20°C/20–40°F. Since ovens vary, you should check
with your manufacturer's instruction book for guidance.
The nutritional analysis given for each recipe is calculated
per portion (i.e. serving or item), unless otherwise stated.
If the recipe gives a range, such as Serves 4–6, then the
nutritional analysis will be for the smaller portion size,
i.e. 6 servings. The analysis does not include optional
ingredients, such as salt added to taste.
Medium (US large) eggs are used unless otherwise stated.
Front cover shows red gooseberry jelly (left) and rhubarb
and mint jelly (right) – for recipes, see pages 32–3.

PUBLISHER'S NOTE

Contents

Introduction

Preserving fruits and vegetables is one of the oldest of the culinary arts. Once essential for survival, it remains a delicious way to store seasonal vegetables or fruits.

AN AGE-OLD TECHNIQUE

Preserving was one of the earliest skills acquired by humankind during the cold winter months when fresh food was scarce. Sun and wind were the first natural agents to be used: when fruits and vegetables were laid out in the hot sun or hung in the wind to dry, they were found to last longer than fresh produce and were lighter and easier to carry. In colder, damp climates, smoke and fire were used to hasten the drying process.

These discoveries meant that travelling to new territories became easier and new settlements were built where it was feasible for people to both grow and store food. It wasn't long before early humans found that salt was a powerful dehydrator, far more reliable than the natural elements of sun and wind. Salt soon became a highly prized commodity – wars were even fought over it. In fact, sometimes the salt was more valuable than the food it preserved, hence the saying that something is not worth its salt.

The preservative properties of vinegar and alcohol were discovered around the same time as those of salt, and people also realized that food could be flavoured while it was being preserved. Vinegar, which creates an acid environment that contaminants cannot live in, was used for preserving worldwide.

Cane sugar was introduced to Europe from the West Indies in the 16th century, and became a sought-after ingredient. Soon the demand for it became so great that it encouraged the rise of colonialism and the slave trade. In the 18th century, beetroot (beet), which had always been enjoyed as a vegetable, began to be cultivated specifically for its sugar content. Eventually sugar became plentiful and cheap, and the liking for sweet preserves started to grow.

BELOW: *Rich, fruity chutneys were first made in India and became popular in Britain in the 19th century.*

ABOVE: *Bottling fruits in flavoured syrups was one of the earliest ways that sugar was used for preserving.*

ABOVE: *Preserving seasonal fruits like the apples in this jelly meant that they were available all year round.*

ABOVE: *Nowadays jams and conserves are made with a huge range of ingredients and flavourings.*

It was during the 19th century that the practice of preserving foods really came into its own and was considered to be a skilled craft. Many of the recipes we use today are based on those that first appeared in cookbooks during that era. Thrifty housewives took pride in filling their capacious pantries with bottles and jars of preserves made from summer and autumn fruits while they were plentiful. These were then enjoyed during the lean winter months to supplement their diet, which would otherwise have consisted mainly of salted meats and root vegetables.

In the 20th century, preserving became less fashionable. Many homes had less storage space and, as the range and use of commercially prepared foods and preserves

increased, stocks of home-made preserves were no longer needed or desirable. Imported produce meant that many fruits and vegetables were available all year round. By the middle of the century, refrigerators could be found in most homes, followed by freezers in the 1960s and 70s, and during those decades freezing became the preferred way of preserving fruit and vegetables and the old-fashioned techniques became less popular.

PRESERVE-MAKING TODAY

Nowadays, the art of preserving is coming back into its own, not because food needs to be processed to make it keep for long periods but for reasons of quality and variety. Improved travel and communication have increased knowledge of

preserves from around the world and more unusual varieties of fruits, vegetables and flavouring ingredients are now readily available.

This book contains a detailed reference section showing how to make sweet and savoury preserves. All the main techniques are shown, including making jams, jellies and marmalades; bottling; pickling; making chutneys and relishes; and drying. There is also a full-colour guide to ingredients – from seasonal fruits and vegetables to flavourings and preservatives.

The recipe collection includes a fantastic range of traditional and contemporary ideas that will prove to be an inspiration and pleasure to both the novice jam-maker and the experienced preserver.

Marmalades

These classic preserves fall somewhere between a jam and a jelly and are traditionally served for breakfast. They can be tart and bitter with thick-cut shreds of peel, or sweet with thinly cut zest, but the rind must be cooked until it is very tender. All the recipes in this chapter will keep for at least a year.

Ruby red grapefruit marmalade

If you prefer a really tangy marmalade, grapefruit is the perfect choice. To achieve a wonderfully red-blushed preserve, look for the red variety rather than pink.

MAKES ABOUT 1.8KG/4LB

900g/2lb ruby red grapefruit, washed
1 lemon, washed
1.2 litres/2 pints/5 cups water
1.3kg/3lb/6½ cups sugar, warmed

1 Remove the rind from the fruit using a vegetable peeler. Halve the fruit and squeeze the juice into a pan, reserving all the pips (seeds). Put the pips and fruit membranes in a muslin (cheesecloth) bag and add to the pan. Discard the shells.

2 Using a sharp knife, cut the grapefruit and lemon rind into thin or coarse shreds, as preferred, and place in the pan. Add the water to the pan and bring to the boil. Cover and simmer for 2 hours, or until the rind is very tender.

3 Remove the muslin bag from the pan, leave to cool, then squeeze it over the pan. Add the sugar and stir over a low heat until it has dissolved. Bring to the boil, then boil rapidly for 10–15 minutes, or to setting point (105°C/220°F).

4 Remove the pan from the heat. Skim off any scum using a slotted spoon. Leave to cool for about 10 minutes, then stir and pour into warmed sterilized jars. Seal, then label when cold.

Nutritional information per quantity: Energy 5392kcal/22,987kJ; Protein 13.7g; Carbohydrate 1419.7g, of which sugars 1419.7g; Fat 0.9g, of which saturates 0g; Cholesterol 0mg; Calcium 896mg; Fibre 11.7g; Sodium 105mg.

Pink grapefruit and cranberry marmalade

Cranberries give this glorious marmalade an extra tartness and a full fruit flavour, as well as an inimitable vibrant colour. The resulting preserve makes a lively choice for breakfast.

MAKES ABOUT 2.25KG/5LB

675g/1½lb pink grapefruit
juice and pips (seeds) of 2 lemons
900ml/1½ pints/3¾ cups water
225g/8oz/2 cups cranberries
1.3kg/3lb/6½ cups sugar, warmed

1 Wash, halve and quarter the grapefruit, then slice them thinly, reserving the pips (seeds) and any juice that runs out. Tie the grapefruit and lemon pips in a muslin (cheesecloth) bag and place in a pan with the grapefruit slices, lemon juice and water. Bring to the boil, then cover and simmer gently for 1½–2 hours, or until the rind is tender. Remove the muslin bag, leave to cool, then squeeze over the pan.

2 Add the cranberries to the pan. Simmer for 15–20 minutes, or until they have popped and softened. Add the sugar and stir over a low heat until it has completely dissolved. Bring to the boil and boil rapidly for about 10 minutes, or until setting point is reached (105°C/220°F).

3 Remove the pan from the heat and skim off any scum from the surface using a slotted spoon. Leave to cool for 10 minutes, then stir and pour into warmed sterilized jars. Seal, then label when the marmalade is cold.

Nutritional information per quantity: Energy 5403kcal/23,043kJ; Protein 12.6g; Carbohydrate 1424.4g, of which sugars 1424.4g; Fat 0.9g, of which saturates 0g; Cholesterol 0mg; Calcium 853mg; Fibre 12.4g; Sodium 103mg.

Lemon and ginger marmalade

This combination of lemon and ginger produces a really zesty and versatile preserve, perfect served on toast at any time of day. It is also excellent added to meat glazes.

MAKES ABOUT 1.8KG/4LB

1.2kg/2¹/₂lb lemons
150g/5oz fresh root ginger, peeled and finely grated
1.2 litres/2 pints/5 cups water
900g/2lb/4¹/₂ cups sugar, warmed

1 Quarter and slice the lemons. Tie the pips (seeds) in a muslin (cheesecloth) bag and place in a preserving pan with the lemons, ginger and water. Bring to the boil, cover with a lid and simmer for 2 hours, or until the fruit is tender.

2 Remove the muslin bag from the pan, leave to cool then squeeze over the pan to release all the juice and pectin. Stir in the sugar over a low heat until dissolved, then increase the heat and boil for 5–10 minutes, or until setting point is reached (105°C/220°F).

3 Remove the pan from the heat and skim off any scum from the surface using a slotted spoon.

4 Leave to cool for 5 minutes, stir, then pour into warmed sterilized jars and seal. When cold, label and store in a cool place.

Nutritional information per quantity: Energy 3785kcal/16,122kJ; Protein 17.3g; Carbohydrate 980.3g, of which sugars 980.3g; Fat 3.9g, of which saturates 1.2g; Cholesterol 0mg; Calcium 1559mg; Fibre 1.6g; Sodium 204mg.

Orange and coriander marmalade

This traditional marmalade made with bitter Seville oranges has the added zing of warm, spicy coriander. Cut the orange rind into thin or coarse shreds, according to taste.

MAKES ABOUT 1.8KG/4LB

675g/1¹/₂lb Seville (Temple) oranges
2 lemons
15ml/1 tbsp crushed coriander seeds
1.5 litres/2³/₄pints/6¹/₄ cups water
900g/2lb/4¹/₂ cups sugar, warmed

1 Cut the oranges and lemons in half and squeeze out all the juice. Place the orange and lemon pips (seeds) in a muslin (cheesecloth) bag. Using a sharp knife, cut the rind into shreds and place in a preserving pan with the juice.

2 Add the coriander seeds to the bag and place in the pan with the water. Bring to the boil, cover and simmer for 2 hours, or until the mixture has reduced by half and the peel is soft. Remove the bag from the pan, cool, then squeeze it over the pan to release the juices and pectin.

3 Add the sugar and stir over a low heat until dissolved. Bring to the boil and boil rapidly for 5–10 minutes, or to setting point (105°C/220°F). Remove the pan from the heat. Skim off any scum from the surface using a slotted spoon. Cool for 5 minutes, stir then pour into warmed sterilized jars. Seal, then label when cold.

Nutritional information per quantity: Energy 3839kcal/16,377kJ; Protein 14.1g; Carbohydrate 1003.1g, of which sugars 997.9g; Fat 2.6g, of which saturates 0.3g; Cholesterol 0mg; Calcium 821mg; Fibre 11.5g; Sodium 93mg.

Orange and whisky marmalade

Adding whisky to orange marmalade gives it a fantastic warmth and flavour. The whisky is stirred in after the marmalade is cooked, to retain its strength and slightly bitter edge.

MAKES ABOUT 2.25KG/5LB

900g/2lb Seville (Temple) oranges
juice and pips (seeds) of 1 large lemon
1.2 litres/2 pints/5 cups water
1.5kg/3lb 6oz/7½ cups sugar, warmed
60ml/4 tbsp whisky

1 Scrub the oranges and halve them. Squeeze the juice into a pan, reserving the pips (seeds) and any membranes. Place these in a muslin (cheesecloth) bag with the lemon pips and add to the juice.

2 Slice the orange rind and put in the pan with the water. Bring to the boil, then cover and simmer for 2 hours, or until the rind is very tender. Remove the bag from the pan, leave to cool, then squeeze over the pan to release any juice and pectin.

3 Add the sugar to the pan and stir over a low heat until completely dissolved. Increase the heat and boil for 5–10 minutes or until setting point is reached (105°C/220°F).

4 Remove the pan from the heat and skim off any scum from the surface using a slotted spoon. Stir in the whisky, then cool for 5 minutes. Stir, then pour the marmalade into warmed sterilized jars. Seal, then label when cold. Store in a cool dark place.

Nutritional information per quantity: Energy 5588kcal/23,826kJ; Protein 16.4g; Carbohydrate 1435g, of which sugars 1435g; Fat 0.9g, of which saturates 0g; Cholesterol 0mg; Calcium 1112mg; Fibre 15.3g; Sodium 123mg.

St Clement's marmalade

This classic preserve made from oranges and lemons has a lovely citrus tang. It has a light, refreshing flavour and is perfect for serving for breakfast, spread on toasted bread.

MAKES ABOUT 2.25KG/5LB

450g/1lb Seville (Temple) oranges
450g/1lb sweet oranges
4 lemons
1.5 litres/2¹⁄₂ pints/6¹⁄₄ cups water
1.2kg/2¹⁄₂ lb/5¹⁄₂ cups sugar, warmed

1 Wash the Seville oranges, sweet oranges and lemons, then cut them in half. Squeeze all of the juice into a large pan. Tie the pips (seeds) with the membranes in a muslin (cheesecloth) bag, then shred the orange and lemon rind and add it to the pan.

2 Add the water to the pan, bring to the boil, cover and leave to simmer for 2 hours. Remove the muslin bag, leave to cool, then squeeze any liquid back into the pan.

3 Add the warmed sugar to the pan and stir over a low heat until the sugar has dissolved. Bring the mixture to the boil and then boil it rapidly for about 15 minutes or until the marmalade reaches setting point (105°C/220°F).

4 Remove from the heat and skim off any scum from the surface. Leave to cool for 5 minutes, stir, then pour into warmed sterilized jars and seal. When cold, label, then store in a cool, dark place.

Nutritional information per quantity: Energy 5061kcal/21,594kJ; Protein 15.9g; Carbohydrate 1330.5g, of which sugars 1330.5g; Fat 0.9g, of which saturates 0g; Cholesterol 0mg; Calcium 1059mg; Fibre 15.3g; Sodium 117mg.

Oxford marmalade

The characteristic caramel colour and rich flavour of a traditional Oxford marmalade are obtained by cutting the fruit coarsely and cooking it for several hours before adding the sugar.

MAKES ABOUT 2.25KG/5LB

900g/2lb Seville (Temple) oranges
1.75 litres/3 pints/7¹/₂ cups water
1.3kg/3lb/6¹/₂ cups sugar, warmed

1 Scrub the orange skins, then remove the rind using a vegetable peeler. Thickly slice the rind and put in a large pan.

2 Chop the fruit, reserving the pips (seeds), and add to the pan, with the water. Tie the pips in a piece of muslin (cheesecloth) and add to the pan. Bring to the boil, then cover and simmer for 2 hours. Add more water during cooking to maintain the same volume. Remove from the heat and leave overnight.

3 The next day, remove the muslin bag, squeezing well, and return the pan to the heat. Bring to the boil, cover and simmer for 1 hour. Add the warmed sugar, then bring to the boil, stirring until the sugar has dissolved. Increase the heat and boil for 15 minutes, or until setting point is reached (105°C/220°F).

4 Remove from the heat and skim off any scum from the surface. Leave to cool for about 5 minutes, stir, then pour into warmed sterilized jars and seal. When cold, label, then store in a cool, dark place.

Nutritional information per quantity: Energy 5455kcal/23,275kJ; Protein 16.4g; Carbohydrate 1435g, of which sugars 1435g; Fat 0.9g, of which saturates 0g; Cholesterol 0mg; Calcium 1112mg; Fibre 15.3g; Sodium 123mg.

Tangerine and lemon grass marmalade

The subtle flavours of lemon grass and kaffir lime leaves add an exotic edge to this delicious marmalade. You can also stir in some thinly shredded lime leaves before bottling.

MAKES ABOUT 1.8KG/4LB

900g/2lb tangerines, washed and halved
juice and pips (seeds) of 2 Seville
   (Temple) oranges
900ml/1¹/₂ pints/3³/₄ cups water
2 lemon grass sticks, halved and crushed
3 kaffir lime leaves
900g/2lb/4¹/₂ cups sugar, warmed

1 Using a sharp knife, slice the tangerines thinly, reserving the pips (seeds). Place the sliced fruit in a preserving pan, along with juice from the Seville oranges and the measured water.

2 Tie all the pips, lemon grass and lime leaves in a piece of muslin (cheesecloth) and add to the pan. Boil, then simmer for 1¹/₂–2 hours, or until the tangerine rind is soft. Remove the bag, leave to cool, then squeeze over the pan.

3 Stir in the sugar over a low heat until completely dissolved, then boil for 5–10 minutes, or to setting point (105°C/220°F).

4 Remove the pan from the heat and then skim off any scum from the surface using a slotted spoon. Leave to cool for 5 minutes, then stir and pour into warmed sterilized jars. Seal, then label when cold.

Nutritional information per quantity: Energy 3935kcal/16,768kJ; Protein 14.8g; Carbohydrate 1029.5g, of which sugars 1029.5g; Fat 1.1g, of which saturates 0g; Cholesterol 0mg; Calcium 949mg; Fibre 15.1g; Sodium 82mg.

Spiced pumpkin marmalade

The bright orange colour and warm flavour of this marmalade are guaranteed to banish the winter blues. The addition of pumpkin gives the preserve more body and a lovely, satisfying texture. It's perfect for spreading on hot buttered toast or serving with warm croissants.

MAKES ABOUT 2.75KG/6LB

900g/2lb Seville (Temple) oranges,
    washed and halved
450g/1lb lemons, halved and
    thinly sliced, pips (seeds) reserved
2 cinnamon sticks
2.5cm/1in piece fresh root ginger,
    peeled and thinly sliced

1.5ml/¼ tsp grated nutmeg
1.75 litres/3 pints/7½ cups water
800g/1¾lb squash or pumpkin,
    peeled, seeds (pips) removed and
    thinly sliced
1.3kg/3lb/6½ cups sugar, warmed

1 Squeeze the juice from the oranges and pour into a preserving pan. Remove the white membranes and reserve with the pips.

2 Thinly slice the orange rind and place in the pan, along with the sliced lemons. Tie the orange and lemon pips and membranes in a muslin (cheesecloth) bag with the spices and add to the pan with the water. Bring to the boil, then cover and simmer for 1 hour.

3 Add the pumpkin to the pan and continue cooking for 1–1½ hours. Remove the muslin bag, leave to cool, then squeeze over the pan.

4 Stir in the sugar over a low heat until completely dissolved. Bring to the boil, then boil rapidly for 15 minutes, or until the marmalade becomes thick and reaches setting point (105°C/220°F). Stir once or twice to ensure the marmalade does not stick to the pan.

5 Remove the pan from the heat and skim off any scum. Leave to cool for 5 minutes, then stir and pour into warmed sterilized jars. Cover the surface of the preserve with wax discs, then seal. Label when the marmalade is cold and store in a cool, dark place.

Nutritional information per quantity: Energy 5645kcal/24,071kJ; Protein 26.5g; Carbohydrate 1467g, of which sugars 1463g; Fat 3.9g, of which saturates 1.2g; Cholesterol 0mg; Calcium 1726mg; Fibre 23.3g; Sodium 145mg.

Clementine and liqueur marmalade

Small, tart clementines make a particularly full-flavoured preserve, which can be put to a wide variety of culinary uses. It is superlative served with smooth ripe Brie and crisp crackers.

MAKES ABOUT 1.8KG/4LB

900g/2lb clementines, washed and
    halved
juice and pips (seeds) of 2 lemons
900ml/1¹/₂ pints/3³/₄ cups water
900g/2lb/4¹/₂ cups sugar, warmed
60ml/4 tbsp Grand Marnier or Cointreau

1 Slice the clementines, reserving any pips. Tie the pips in a muslin (cheesecloth) bag with the lemon pips and place in a large pan with the sliced fruit.

2 Add the lemon juice and water to the fruit and bring to the boil. Cover the pan, reduce the heat and simmer for 1¹/₂ hours, until the rind is very tender. Remove the muslin bag, cool, then squeeze over the pan.

3 Stir in the sugar over a low heat until dissolved, then bring to the boil and cook for 5–10 minutes, or until the mixture reaches setting point (105°C/220°F).

4 Remove the pan from the heat and skim off any scum from the surface. Leave to cool for 5 minutes, then stir in the liqueur and pour into warmed sterilized jars. Seal, then label when cold.

Nutritional information per quantity: Energy 4036kcal/17,210kJ; Protein 12.6g; Carbohydrate 1038.5g, of which sugars 1038.5g; Fat 0.9g, of which saturates 0g; Cholesterol 0mg; Calcium 759mg; Fibre 10.8g; Sodium 97mg.

Pomelo and pineapple marmalade

Pomelos are slightly larger than grapefruits and have lime-green skin and a sharp, refreshing flavour. They are delicious combined with tangy pineapple.

MAKES ABOUT 2.75KG/6LB

2 pomelos, washed and halved
900ml/1½ pints/3¾ cups water
2 x 425g/15oz cans crushed pineapple
    in fruit juice
900g/2lb/4½ cups sugar, warmed

1 Squeeze out the pomelo juice, reserving any pips (seeds), and pour into a large pan. Tie the membranes and any excess pith in muslin (cheesecloth) with the pips. Slice the peel thinly and add to the pan with the muslin bag and water.

2 Bring to the boil, cover and simmer for 1½–2 hours, stirring occasionally, or until the fruit is soft. Add the pineapple and juice and simmer for 30 minutes.

3 Remove the bag from the pan, cool, then squeeze over the pan. Add the sugar and stir over a low heat until it has dissolved. Increase the heat and then boil for 10 minutes, or to setting point (105°C/220°F).

4 Remove the pan from the heat and skim off any scum from the surface. Cool for 10 minutes, then stir and pour into warmed sterilized jars. Seal, then label the jars when they are cold.

Nutritional information per quantity: Energy 4042kcal/17,233kJ; Protein 10.1g; Carbohydrate 1065.3g, of which sugars 1065.3g; Fat 0.4g, of which saturates 0g; Cholesterol 0mg; Calcium 633mg; Fibre 9.2g; Sodium 74mg.

Peach and kumquat marmalade

Combined with sweet, scented peaches, kumquats make a wonderful, fresh-tasting preserve. This lovely marmalade has a jam-like consistency and is great at any time of day.

MAKES ABOUT 1.8KG/4LB

675g/1¹/₂lb kumquats, thinly sliced, pips (seeds) and
    juice reserved
juice and pips of 1 lime
900g/2lb peaches, skinned and thinly sliced, skins reserved
900ml/1¹/₂ pints/3³/₄ cups water
900g/2lb/4¹/₂ cups sugar, warmed

1 Tie the kumquat and lime pips, and the peach skins, in a muslin (cheesecloth) bag. Put them in a pan with the kumquats and their juice, lime juice and water. Bring to the boil, then cover and simmer for 50 minutes.

2 Add the peaches to the pan, bring to the boil, then simmer for 40–50 minutes, or until the fruit is very soft. Remove the bag, cool, then squeeze over the pan.

3 Add the sugar to the pan and stir over a low heat until it has dissolved. Bring the mixture to the boil, then boil rapidly for about 15 minutes, stirring occasionally, to setting point (105°C/220°F). Remove the pan from the heat and skim off any scum from the surface using a slotted spoon.

4 Leave to cool for 5–10 minutes, then stir and pour into warmed sterilized jars. Seal, then label when the jars are cold. Store in a cool, dark place.

Nutritional information per quantity: Energy 4093kcal/17,474kJ; Protein 19.6g; Carbohydrate 1067.6g, of which sugars 1067.6g; Fat 1.6g, of which saturates 0g; Cholesterol 0mg; Calcium 749mg; Fibre 21.6g; Sodium 90mg.

Apricot and orange marmalade

Serve this sweet marmalade with warm croissants and strong coffee for a leisurely weekend breakfast. The combination of oranges and rich-tasting apricots is a winner.

MAKES ABOUT 1.5KG/3LB 5OZ

2 Seville (Temple) oranges, washed and quartered
1 lemon, washed and quartered
1.2 litres/2 pints/5 cups water
900g/2lb apricots, stoned (pitted) and thinly sliced
900g/2lb/4¹/₂ cups sugar, warmed

1 Remove the pips (seeds) from the citrus fruit and tie in a muslin (cheesecloth) bag.

2 Finely chop the oranges and lemons in a food processor and put in a large pan with the muslin bag and water. Bring the mixture to the boil, then simmer, covered, for 1 hour.

3 Add the apricots to the pan, bring to the boil, then simmer for 30–40 minutes, or until very tender.

4 Add the sugar to the pan and stir over a low heat until the sugar has dissolved. Bring to the boil, then boil rapidly for 15 minutes, stirring occasionally, until setting point is reached (105°C/220°F).

5 Remove the pan from the heat and skim off any scum from the surface using a slotted spoon. Leave to cool for about 5 minutes, then stir and pour into warmed sterilized jars. Seal, then label when cold. Store in a cool place.

Nutritional information per quantity: Energy 3936kcal/16,809kJ; Protein 15.9g; Carbohydrate 1030.8g, of which sugars 1030.8g; Fat 1.2g, of which saturates 0g; Cholesterol 0mg; Calcium 753mg; Fibre 20.4g; Sodium 87mg.

Jellies

Sparkling, jewel-like sweet fruit jellies

make a wonderful alternative to jams and

conserves, as well as a delicious

condiment to serve with savoury foods

such as meat, fish or cheese. The fruit is

cooked gently for as short a time as

possible, then strained to obtain the clear

liquid which forms the jelly.

Hedgerow jelly

In the autumn, hedgerows are laden with damsons, blackberries and elderberries and it is well worth spending an afternoon in the countryside picking fruit to make into this delightful jelly.

MAKES ABOUT 1.3KG/3LB

450g/1lb/4 cups damsons, washed
450g/1lb/4 cups blackberries, washed
225g/8oz/2 cups raspberries
225g/8oz/2 cups elderberries, washed

juice and pips (seeds) of 2 large lemons
about 1.3kg/3lb/6½ cups preserving
or granulated (white) sugar, warmed

1 Put the fruit, lemon juice and pips in a large pan. Pour over just enough water to cover. Put a lid on the pan, bring to the boil, then simmer for 1 hour.

2 Mash the fruit and leave to cool slightly. Pour into a scalded jelly bag suspended over a non-metallic bowl and leave to drain overnight.

3 Measure the strained juice into a preserving pan. Add 450g/1lb/2¼ cups sugar for every 600ml/1 pint/2½ cups strained fruit juice.

4 Heat the mixture, stirring, over a low heat until the sugar has dissolved. Increase the heat and boil rapidly without stirring for 10–15 minutes, or until the jelly reaches setting point (105°C/220°F).

5 Remove the pan from the heat and skim off any scum using a slotted spoon. Ladle into warmed sterilized jars and seal. Leave to cool, then label and store.

Nutritional information per quantity: Energy 5229kcal/22,306kJ; Protein 9.3g; Carbohydrate 1382.8g, of which sugars 1382.8g; Fat 0.4g, of which saturates 0g; Cholesterol 0mg; Calcium 799mg; Fibre 8.6g; Sodium 86mg.

Mulberry jelly

Deep red mulberries are not often available but if you have access to a tree you will find they make the most wonderful jellies and jams. For a good set, pick the fruits when they are red.

MAKES ABOUT 900G/2LB

900g/2lb/8 cups unripe red mulberries
grated rind and juice of 1 lemon
600ml/1 pint/2¹/₂ cups water
about 900g/2lb/4¹/₂ cups preserving or
granulated (white) sugar, warmed

1 Put the mulberries in a pan with the lemon rind and juice and the water. Bring to the boil, cover and simmer for 1 hour, then remove from the heat and leave to cool. Pour the fruit into a scalded jelly bag suspended over a non-metallic bowl and leave to drain overnight.

2 Measure the strained juice into a preserving pan. Add 450g/1lb/2¹/₄ cups sugar for every 600ml/1 pint/2¹/₂ cups fruit juice.

3 Heat the mixture over a low heat, stirring, until the sugar has completely dissolved. Increase the heat and then boil rapidly, without stirring, for 5–10 minutes or to setting point (105°C/220°F).

4 Skim off any scum from the surface of the jelly using a slotted spoon. Ladle into warmed sterilized jars, cover and seal. When the jars are completely cool, label, then store in a cool, dark place.

Nutritional information per quantity: Energy 3621kcal/15,456kJ; Protein 8.7g; Carbohydrate 954.3g, of which sugars 954.3g; Fat 0.9g, of which saturates 0.3g; Cholesterol 0mg; Calcium 552mg; Fibre 7.5g; Sodium 63mg.

Scented geranium and pear jelly

This jelly uses the leaves of scented geranium to give an aromatic lift to the pears. Use rose-scented leaves if you have them, otherwise add a couple of drops of rose water to the strained juice.

MAKES ABOUT 900G/2LB

900g/2lb Comice pears, washed and
   coarsely chopped with skins and
   cores intact
7 rose-scented geranium leaves, plus
   extra for storing
juice and pips (seeds) of 1 lemon
60ml/4 tbsp clear honey
900ml/1½ pints/3¾ cups water
about 900g/2lb/4½ cups preserving
   or granulated (white) sugar, warmed

1 Put the pears, geranium leaves, lemon juice, honey and water in a large pan. Bring to the boil, then cover and simmer for 1 hour.

2 Remove the pan from the heat and cool slightly. Pour the fruit into a scalded jelly bag suspended over a non-metallic bowl and drain overnight.

3 Measure the strained juice into a preserving pan. Add 450g/1lb/2¼ cups warmed sugar for every 600ml/1 pint/2½ cups juice. Heat, stirring, over a low heat until the sugar has dissolved. Increase the heat and boil rapidly, without stirring, for 10 minutes, or to setting point (105°C/220°F).

4 Remove from the heat and skim off any scum. Place a blanched geranium leaf into each warmed sterilized jar, then add the jelly. Cover, seal and label.

Nutritional information per quantity: Energy 3851kcal/16,424kJ; Protein 5.7g; Carbohydrate 1019.3g, of which sugars 1019.3g; Fat 0.3g, of which saturates 0g; Cholesterol 0mg; Calcium 516mg; Fibre 7.3g; Sodium 70mg.

Citrus thyme jelly

You can vary the sharpness of this jelly by altering the proportions of fruit. Use more oranges and fewer lemons and limes to obtain a milder, sweeter-tasting jelly.

MAKES ABOUT 1.3KG/3LB

675g/1¹/₂lb lemons
675g/1¹/₂lb limes
450g/1lb oranges
2 bay leaves

2 litres/3¹/₂ pints/8³/₄ cups water
about 800g/1³/₄lb/4 cups preserving
   or granulated (white) sugar
60ml/4 tbsp fresh thyme leaves

1 Wash all the fruit, then cut into small pieces. Place the fruit in a large heavy pan with the bay leaves and pour over the water.

2 Bring the mixture to the boil, then reduce the heat, cover and simmer for 1 hour, or until pulpy. Discard the bay leaves, then pour the fruit and juices into a sterilized jelly bag suspended over a large bowl. Leave to drain for 3 hours, or until the juices stop dripping.

3 Measure the juice into the cleaned pan, adding 450g/1lb/2¹/₄ cups sugar for every 600ml/1 pint/2¹/₂ cups juice. Heat gently until the sugar has dissolved. Bring to the boil, then boil rapidly for about 10 minutes, or until setting point is reached (105°C/220°F). Remove the pan from the heat.

4 Skim any scum off the surface with a slotted spoon, then stir in the thyme leaves. Leave to cool for a few minutes until a thin skin forms, then gently stir again to make sure the thyme is evenly distributed.

5 Pour the jelly into warmed sterilized jars. Cover, allow to cool and then seal. Store in a cool, dark place and use within 1 year. Once opened, store in the refrigerator and eat within 3 months.

Nutritional information per quantity: Energy 3154kcal/13,455kJ; Protein 4.2g; Carbohydrate 836.1g, of which sugars 836.1g; Fat 0.1g, of which saturates 0g; Cholesterol 0mg; Calcium 434mg; Fibre 0.2g; Sodium 50mg.

Rhubarb and mint jelly

This delicious jelly is very pretty, specked with tiny pieces of chopped fresh mint. It has a sharp, tangy flavour and is fabulous spread on toast or crumpets at tea time.

MAKES ABOUT 2KG/4½LB

1kg/2¼lb rhubarb
about 1.3kg/3lb/6½ cups preserving
    or granulated (white) sugar, warmed
large bunch fresh mint
30ml/2 tbsp finely chopped
    fresh mint

1 Using a sharp knife, cut the rhubarb into chunks and place in a large, heavy pan. Pour in just enough water to cover, cover the pan with a lid and then cook until the rhubarb is soft.

2 Remove the pan from the heat and leave to cool slightly. Pour the stewed fruit and juices into a scalded jelly bag suspended over a non-metallic bowl and leave to drain overnight.

3 Measure the strained juice into a preserving pan and add 450g/1lb/2¼ cups warmed sugar for each 600ml/ 1 pint/2½ cups strained juice.

4 Add the bunch of mint to the pan. Bring to the boil, stirring until the sugar has dissolved. Boil to setting point (105°C/220°F). Remove the mint.

5 Leave to stand for 10 minutes, stir in the chopped mint, then pot and seal. Label when cold.

Nutritional information per quantity: Energy 5165kcal/22,039kJ; Protein 11.1g; Carbohydrate 1363.5g, of which sugars 1360.9g; Fat 0.6g, of which saturates 0g; Cholesterol 0mg; Calcium 1073mg; Fibre 4.2g; Sodium 94mg.

Red gooseberry jelly

This jelly has a rich red colour and is perfect for spreading on toast at any time of the day. Choose small, dark-red gooseberries for the best colour and flavour.

MAKES ABOUT 2KG/4½LB

1.3kg/3lb/12 cups red gooseberries
2 red-skinned eating apples, washed and chopped
    with skins and cores intact
2.5cm/1in piece fresh root ginger, sliced
about 1.3kg/3lb/6½ cups preserving
    or granulated (white) sugar, warmed

1 Put the fruit and ginger in a pan and pour over just enough water to cover the fruit. Bring to the boil, then reduce the heat, cover and simmer for 45 minutes.

2 Remove from the heat, cool slightly, then pour the fruit and juices into a scalded jelly bag suspended over a non-metallic bowl and leave to drain overnight.

3 Measure the strained juice into a preserving pan and add 450g/1lb/2¼ cups warmed sugar for every 600ml/ 1 pint/2½ cups juice. Stir over a low heat until the sugar has dissolved. Boil for about 10 minutes, or to setting point (105°C/220°F). Skim off any scum, then pot, seal and label when cold.

COOK'S TIP
The amount of pectin in gooseberries diminishes as the fruit ripens so select firm, just-ripe fruit when making this jelly to achieve a really good set.

Nutritional information per quantity: Energy 5233kcal/22,327kJ; Protein 11.8g; Carbohydrate 1378.3g, of which sugars 1378.3g; Fat 1.9g, of which saturates 0g; Cholesterol 0mg; Calcium 820mg; Fibre 12.1g; Sodium 89mg.

Roasted red pepper and chilli jelly

The hint of chilli in this glowing red jelly makes it ideal for spicing up hot or cold roast meat, sausages or hamburgers. The jelly is also good stirred into sauces or used as a glaze for poultry.

MAKES ABOUT 900G/2LB

8 red (bell) peppers, quartered and seeded
4 fresh red chillies, halved and seeded
1 onion, roughly chopped
2 garlic cloves, roughly chopped
250ml/8fl oz/1 cup water
250ml/8fl oz/1 cup white wine vinegar
7.5ml/1½ tsp salt
450g/1lb/2¼ cups preserving or granulated (white) sugar
25ml/1½ tbsp powdered pectin

1 Arrange the peppers, skin side up, on a rack in a grill (broiling) pan and grill (broil) until the skins blacken.

2 Put the peppers in a polythene bag until they are cool enough to handle, then remove the skins.

3 Put the red peppers, red chillies, onion, garlic and water in a food processor or blender and process to a purée.

4 Press the purée through a nylon sieve (strainer) set over a bowl, pressing hard with a wooden spoon to extract as much juice as possible. There should be about 750ml/1¼ pints/3 cups. Scrape the purée into a large pan, then stir in the white wine vinegar and salt.

5 In a bowl, combine the warmed sugar and pectin, then stir it into the puréed pepper mixture.

6 Heat the mixture gently, stirring, until the sugar and pectin have dissolved completely, then bring to a rolling boil.

7 Cook the jelly, stirring frequently, for exactly 4 minutes, then remove the pan from the heat.

8 Pour the jelly into warmed, sterilized jars. Leave to cool and set, then cover, label and store.

Nutritional information per quantity:
Energy 2275kcal/9665kJ; Protein 18g; Carbohydrate 571g, of which sugars 565.1g; Fat 6.1g, of which saturates 1.5g; Cholesterol 0mg; Calcium 373mg; Fibre 24.8g; Sodium 89mg.

Lemon grass and ginger jelly

This aromatic jelly is delicious with Asian-style roast meat and poultry such as Chinese crispy duck. It is also the perfect foil for rich fish, especially cold smoked trout or mackerel.

MAKES ABOUT 900G/2LB

2 lemon grass stalks
1.5 litres/2¹/₂ pints/6¹/₄ cups water
1.3kg/3lb lemons, washed and cut
    into small pieces
50g/2oz fresh root ginger, unpeeled,
    thinly sliced
about 450g/1lb/2¹/₄ cups preserving
    or granulated (white) sugar

1 Using a rolling pin, bruise the lemon grass, then chop roughly, Put in a preserving pan and pour over the water.

2 Add the lemons and ginger to the pan. Bring to the boil, then reduce the heat, cover and simmer for 1 hour, or until the lemons are pulpy.

3 Pour the fruit and juices into a sterilized jelly bag suspended over a large bowl. Drain for at least 3 hours, or until the juice stops dripping. Measure the spiced lemon juice into the cleaned preserving pan, then add 450g/1lb/2¹/₄ cups preserving sugar for every 600ml/ 1 pint/2¹/₂ cups juice.

4 Heat the mixture gently, stirring occasionally, until all of the sugar has dissolved completely. Bring to the boil and boil rapidly for about 10 minutes until the jelly reaches setting point (105°C/220°F).

5 Remove the preserving pan from the heat and carefully skim any scum off the surface of the jelly using a slotted spoon.

6 Pour the into warmed sterilized jars, then cover and seal. Label when cold. Store the jars in a cool, dark place and use within 1 year. Once opened, keep in the refrigerator and consume within 3 months.

Nutritional information per quantity:
Energy 1715kcal/7304kJ; Protein 27.4g; Carbohydrate 417.1g, of which sugars 231.8g; Fat 4.5g, of which saturates 0.7g; Cholesterol 0mg; Calcium 63mg; Fibre 14.4g; Sodium 41mg.

Rosehip and apple jelly

This economical yet truly delicious jelly is made with windfall apples and wild rosehips. It is full of flavour, and excellent spread on freshly toasted crumpets or scones. Rosehips are a great source of vitamin C, and can even help with the relief of headaches or dizziness.

MAKES ABOUT 2KG/4½LB

1kg/2¼ lb windfall apples, peeled, trimmed and quartered
450g/1lb firm, ripe rosehips

about 1.3kg/3lb/6½ cups preserving or granulated (white) sugar, warmed

1 Place the quartered apples in a large pan with just enough water to cover, plus 300ml/½ pint/1¼ cups of extra water.

2 Bring the mixture to the boil and cook gently until the apples soften and turn to a pulp. Meanwhile, chop the rosehips coarsely. Add the rosehips to the pan with the apple and simmer for 10 minutes.

3 Remove from the heat and leave to stand for 10 minutes, then pour the mixture into a scalded jelly bag suspended over a non-metallic bowl and leave to drain overnight.

4 Measure the juice into a preserving pan and bring to the boil. Add 400g/14oz/2 cups warmed sugar for each 600ml/1 pint/2½ cups of liquid. Stir until the sugar has completely dissolved. Boil to setting point (105°C/220°F).

5 Pour the jelly into warmed sterilized jars and seal. Label the jars when the jelly is completely cold, and store in a cool, dark place.

COOK'S TIP
There is no need to remove all the peel from the apples: simply cut out any bruised, damaged or bad areas.

Nutritional information per quantity: Energy 5684kcal/24,259kJ; Protein 8.4g; Carbohydrate 1505.7g, of which sugars 1505.7g; Fat 0.5g, of which saturates 0g; Cholesterol 0mg; Calcium 761mg; Fibre 7.7g; Sodium 94mg.

Quince and coriander jelly

When raw, quinces are inedible but once cooked and sweetened they become aromatic and have a wonderful flavour, which is enhanced here by the addition of warm, spicy coriander seeds.

MAKES ABOUT 900G/2LB

1kg/2¹/₄lb quinces, washed and coarsely
    chopped with skins and cores intact
15ml/1 tbsp coriander seeds
juice and pips (seeds) of 2 large lemons
900ml/1¹/₂ pints/3³/₄ cups water
about 900g/2lb/4¹/₂ cups preserving
    or granulated (white) sugar, warmed

1 Put the quinces in a pan with the coriander seeds, lemon juice and pips, and the water. Bring to the boil, cover and simmer gently for 1¹/₂ hours. Cool slightly, then pour into a scalded jelly bag suspended over a non-metallic bowl. Drain overnight.

2 Measure the strained juice into a preserving pan. Add 450g/1lb/2¹/₄ cups warmed sugar for every 600ml/ 1 pint/2¹/₂ cups juice.

3 Heat gently, stirring, until the sugar has dissolved. Increase the heat and boil rapidly, for 5–10 minutes or until the jelly reaches setting point (105°C/220°F).

4 Remove from the heat and skim off any scum from the surface using a slotted spoon. Ladle the jelly into warmed sterilized jars, cover and seal. When the jelly is cold, label and store in a cool, dark place.

Nutritional information per quantity: Energy 3678kcal/15,687kJ; Protein 5.5g; Carbohydrate 973.5g, of which sugars 973.5g; Fat 0.3g, of which saturates 0g; Cholesterol 0mg; Calcium 513mg; Fibre 7.3g; Sodium 64mg.

Pineapple and passion fruit jelly

This exotic jelly has a wonderful warming glow to its taste and appearance. For the best-flavoured jelly, use a tart-tasting, not too ripe pineapple rather than a very ripe, sweet one.

MAKES ABOUT 900G/2LB

1 large pineapple, peeled, topped and tailed and coarsely chopped
4 passion fruit, halved, with seeds and pulp scooped out
900ml/1¹/₂ pints/3³/₄ cups water
about 900g/2lb/4¹/₂ cups preserving or granulated (white) sugar, warmed

1 Place the pineapple and the passion fruit seeds and pulp in a large pan with the water.

2 Bring to the boil, cover and gently simmer for 1¹/₂ hours. Remove from the heat and leave to cool slightly. Transfer the fruit to a food processor and process briefly.

3 Tip the fruit pulp, and any juices from the pan, into a scalded jelly bag suspended over a non-metallic bowl and leave to drain overnight.

4 Measure the strained juice into a pan and add 450g/1lb/ 2¹/₄ cups preserving sugar for every 600ml/ 1 pint/2¹/₂ cups juice. Heat gently, stirring. When the sugar has dissolved increase the heat and boil rapidly, for 10 minutes, until the jelly reaches setting point (105°C/220°F).

5 Remove from the heat and skim off any scum with a slotted spoon. Ladle into warmed sterilized jars, cover and seal. When cool, label and store in a cool, dark place.

Nutritional information per quantity: Energy 3633kcal/15,504kJ; Protein 5.7g; Carbohydrate 961.6g, of which sugars 961.6g; Fat 0.5g, of which saturates 0g; Cholesterol 0mg; Calcium 515mg; Fibre 2.9g; Sodium 61mg.

Clementine and lemon balm jelly

This sweet, aromatic jelly makes a delicious alternative to marmalade at breakfast. Clementines are the smallest of the tangerine family and have the most zesty flavour.

MAKES ABOUT 900G/2LB

900g/2lb clementines, washed and coarsely chopped
450g/1lb tart cooking apples, coarsely chopped, with skins and cores intact
2 large sprigs of lemon balm or 1 lemon grass stalk, crushed
900ml/1¹/₂ pints/3³/₄ cups water
about 900g/2lb/4¹/₂ cups preserving or granulated (white) sugar, warmed

1 Put the fruit, lemon balm or lemon grass, and water in a large pan. Bring to the boil, cover and simmer for about 1 hour until the fruit is soft. Cool slightly, then pour into a scalded jelly bag over a bowl and leave to drain overnight.

2 Measure the juice into a pan. Add 450g/1lb/2¹/₄ cups sugar for every 600ml/1 pint/2¹/₂ cups juice.

3 Heat gently, stirring until the sugar has dissolved. Increase the heat and boil the mixture, without stirring, for 5–10 minutes, or until the jelly reaches setting point (105°C/220°F).

4 Remove the pan from the heat and skim off any scum using a slotted spoon. Pour into warmed sterilized jars, cover and seal. Label and store in a cool place.

Nutritional information per quantity: Energy 3721kcal/15,877kJ; Protein 7.9g; Carbohydrate 982.6g, of which sugars 982.6g; Fat 0.5g, of which saturates 0g; Cholesterol 0mg; Calcium 585mg; Fibre 6.4g; Sodium 70mg.

Muscat grape and elderflower jelly

The wonderful perfumed flavour of Muscat grapes produces a deliciously fragrant, scented jelly. Do not be tempted to use other grapes because they will not give the same result.

MAKES ABOUT 900G/2LB

900g/2lb/6 cups Muscat grapes, washed and halved
juice and pips (seeds) of 2 lemons
600ml/1 pint/2¹/₂ cups water
30ml/2 tbsp elderflower cordial
about 900g/2lb/4¹/₂ cups preserving or granulated (white) sugar, warmed

1 Place the grapes in a pan with the lemon juice and pips, and water. Bring to the boil, cover and simmer for 1¹/₂ hours. Cool slightly.

2 Mash the grapes, then pour the mixture into a scalded jelly bag suspended over a non-metallic bowl and leave to drain overnight.

3 Measure the juice into the cleaned pan and then pour in the elderflower cordial. Add 450g/1lb/2¹/₄ cups sugar for every 600ml/1 pint/2¹/₂ cups juice. Heat gently, stirring, until the sugar has dissolved. Increase the heat and boil, without stirring, for 5–10 minutes, or until the jelly reaches setting point (105°C/220°F).

4 Remove the pan from the heat and skim off any scum from the surface using a slotted spoon. Ladle into warmed sterilized jars. Cover, seal and label. Store in a cool place.

Nutritional information per quantity: Energy 3778kcal/16,121kJ; Protein 5.8g; Carbohydrate 1000.3g, of which sugars 1000.3g; Fat 0.3g, of which saturates 0g; Cholesterol 0mg; Calcium 523mg; Fibre 2.3g; Sodium 63mg.

Cranberry jelly

This clear, well-flavoured preserve has a tart flavour and is absolutely delicious served with freshly baked scones, toasted tea cakes and crumpets, or as a glaze for fruit tarts.

MAKES ABOUT 900G/2LB

900g/2lb/8 cups cranberries

450g/1lb sweet eating apples, washed
    and chopped with skins and
    cores intact

grated rind and juice of 1 orange

600ml/1 pint/2½ cups water

about 900g/2lb/4½ cups preserving
    or granulated (white) sugar, warmed

1 Put the cranberries and apples in a pan with the orange rind and juice, and water. Bring to the boil, cover and simmer for 1 hour.

2 Remove from the heat, allow to cool slightly then pour the mixture into a scalded jelly bag suspended over a non-metallic bowl and leave to drain overnight. Measure the strained juice into a preserving pan. Add 450g/1lb/2¼ cups sugar for every 600ml/1 pint/ 2½ cups juice.

3 Heat gently, stirring, until the sugar has dissolved. Increase the heat and boil rapidly, without stirring, for 5–10 minutes, or until the jelly reaches setting point (105°C/220°F).

4 Remove from the heat and skim off any scum from the surface using a slotted spoon. Ladle the jelly into warmed sterilized jars, cover and seal. Leave to cool, then label and store in a cool, dark place.

Nutritional information per quantity: Energy 3721kcal/15,884kJ; Protein 6g; Carbohydrate 985g, of which sugars 985g; Fat 0.5g, of which saturates 0g; Cholesterol 0mg; Calcium 497mg; Fibre 8g; Sodium 64mg.

Red plum and cardamom jelly

The fragrance of warm, spicy cardamom combines wonderfully with all varieties of plum –
red plums with a good tart flavour are perfect for making into this sweet, fruity, aromatic jelly.

MAKES ABOUT 1.8KG/4LB

1.8kg/4lb red plums, stoned (pitted)
10ml/2 tsp crushed green
    cardamom pods
600ml/1 pint/2^1/$_2$ cups red grape juice
150ml/^{1}/$_4$ pint/^{2}/$_3$ cup water
about 1.3kg/3lb/6^1/$_2$ cups preserving
    or (white) granulated sugar, warmed

1 Put the plums, cardamom pods, grape juice and water in a large pan. Bring to the boil, then cover and simmer gently for 1 hour. Leave to cool slightly, then pour into a scalded jelly bag suspended over a non-metallic bowl and leave to drain overnight.

2 Measure the strained juice into a preserving pan. Add 450g/1lb/ 2^1/$_4$ cups sugar for every 600ml/ 1 pint/2^1/$_2$ cups strained juice.

3 Heat the mixture over a low heat, stirring constantly, until the sugar has dissolved completely. Increase the heat and boil the mixture, without stirring, for 10–15 minutes, or until the jelly reaches setting point (105°C/220°F).

4 Remove the pan from the heat and skim off any scum. Spoon the jelly into warmed sterilized jars, cover and seal. When cool, label and store in a cool, dark place.

Nutritional information per quantity: Energy 5338kcal/22,783kJ; Protein 10.1g; Carbohydrate 1411.3g, of which sugars 1411.3g; Fat 0.6g, of which saturates 0g; Cholesterol 0mg; Calcium 767mg; Fibre 9.6g; Sodium 90mg.

Red grape, plum and cardamom jelly

Enhance the flavour of roast beef and steaks with a spoonful of deep ruby-coloured jelly. You may need to add a little pectin to the jelly to ensure you achieve a really good set.

MAKES ABOUT 1.3KG/3LB

15ml/1 tbsp cardamom pods
1.8kg/4lb plums, halved and chopped
450g/1lb/3 cups red grapes, halved
600ml/1 pint/2½ cups cold water
350–450ml/12fl oz–¾ pint/1½ cups–
    scant 2 cups pectin stock (optional)
about 1kg/2¼lb/5 cups preserving
    or (white) granulated sugar

1 Remove the cardamom seeds from the pods and crush in a mortar. Put the fruit, cardamom seeds and water in a pan. Bring to the boil and simmer for 30 minutes, or until tender. To check pectin content, spoon 5ml/1 tsp of the juices into a glass. Add 15ml/1 tbsp of methylated spirits (denatured alcohol) and shake gently. If a large and jelly-like clot forms, or two or three smaller clots, the pectin content should be fine. If it is low, add a little pectin stock to the fruit mixture.

2 Pour the fruit into a sterilized jelly bag suspended over a non-metallic bowl. Drain for 3 hours, or until it stops dripping. Measure the juice into a pan, adding 450g/1lb/2¼ cups sugar for every 600ml/1 pint/2½ cups juice.

3 Heat gently, stirring occasionally, until the sugar has completely dissolved. Bring to the boil, then boil for 10 minutes to setting point (105°C/220°F). Remove from the heat. Skim off any scum from the surface, then pour the jelly into warmed sterilized jars, cover and seal. Store in a cool, dark place.

Nutritional information per quantity: Energy 4246kcal/18,126kJ; Protein 9.2g; Carbohydrate 1120.9g, of which sugars 1120.9g; Fat 0.8g, of which saturates 0g; Cholesterol 0mg; Calcium 627mg; Fibre 10.7g; Sodium 75mg.

Quince and rosemary jelly

The amount of water needed for this jelly varies according to the ripeness of the fruit. For a good set, hard, under-ripe quinces should be used because they contain the most pectin.

MAKES ABOUT 900G/2LB

900g/2lb quinces, cut into small pieces,
   with bruised parts removed
900ml–1.2 litres/1¹/₂–2 pints/
   3³/₄–5 cups water
lemon juice (optional)
4 large sprigs of fresh rosemary
about 900g/2lb/4¹/₂ cups preserving
   or (white) granulated sugar

1 Put the chopped quinces in a pan with the water, using the smaller volume of water if they are ripe, and more – plus a little lemon juice – if they are hard. Reserve a few sprigs of rosemary, adding the rest to the pan. Bring to the boil, reduce the heat, cover, and simmer gently until the fruit becomes pulpy. Remove and discard all the rosemary sprigs. Pour into a sterilized jelly bag suspended over a bowl. Leave for 3 hours, or until the juices stop dripping.

2 Measure the drained juice into a pan, adding 450g/1lb/2¹/₄ cups sugar for every 600ml/1 pint/2¹/₂ cups juice. Heat gently over a low heat, until the sugar has dissolved completely. Bring to the boil, then boil rapidly for about 10 minutes until the jelly reaches setting point (105°C/220°F).

3 Remove from the heat. Skim off any scum, then cool for a few minutes until a thin skin forms on the surface. Place a sprig of rosemary in each warmed sterilized jar, then pour in the jelly. Cover and seal when cold. Store in a cool, dark place and use within 1 year.

Nutritional information per quantity: Energy 3666kcal/15,636kJ; Protein 5.4g; Carbohydrate 970.5g, of which sugars 970.5g; Fat 0.3g, of which saturates 0g; Cholesterol 0mg; Calcium 510mg; Fibre 6.6g; Sodium 63mg.

Apple, orange and cider jelly

A spoonful or two of this tangy amber jelly adds a real sparkle to a plate of cold meats, especially ham and pork or rich game pâtés. Tart cooking apples make the best-flavoured jelly, while the addition of cloves gives it a wonderfully warm, spicy taste and aroma.

MAKES ABOUT 1.8KG/4LB

1.3kg/3lb tart cooking apples
4 oranges
4 whole cloves
1.2 litres/2 pints/5 cups sweet cider

about 600ml/1 pint/2½ cups cold water
about 800g/1¾lb/4 cups preserving
   or granulated (white) sugar

1 Wash and chop the apples and oranges, then put in a preserving pan with the cloves, cider and enough water to barely cover the fruit.

2 Bring the fruit mixture to the boil, cover with a lid and simmer gently for 1 hour, stirring occasionally.

3 Pour the fruit and juices into a sterilized jelly bag suspended over a large non-metallic bowl. Leave the mixture to drain for at least 4 hours, or overnight, until the juices have stopped dripping.

4 Measure the juice into the cleaned preserving pan, adding 450g/1lb/2¼ cups sugar for every 600ml/1 pint/2½ cups juice.

5 Heat the mixture gently, stirring, until the sugar has dissolved. Boil rapidly for about 10 minutes until setting point is reached (105°C/220°F). Remove from the heat.

6 Skim any scum off the surface, then pour the jelly into warmed sterilized jars. Cover, seal and label when cold. Store in a cool, dark place and use within 1 year. Once opened, store in the refrigerator and eat within 3 months.

Nutritional information per quantity: Energy 3442kcal/14,691kJ; Protein 10.4g; Carbohydrate 905.2g, of which sugars 905.2g; Fat 0.8g, of which saturates 0g; Cholesterol 0mg; Calcium 671mg; Fibre 13.3g; Sodium 79mg.

Spiced cider and apple jelly

This wonderful spicy jelly has a rich, warming flavour, making it ideal to serve during the cold winter months. Serve as a spread or use it to sweeten apple pies and desserts.

MAKES ABOUT 1.3KG/3LB

900g/2lb tart cooking apples, washed and coarsely chopped with skins and cores intact
900ml/1½ pints/3¾ cups sweet cider juice and pips (seeds) of 2 oranges
1 cinnamon stick
6 whole cloves
150ml/½ pint/⅔ cup water
about 900g/2lb/4½ cups preserving or granulated (white) sugar, warmed

1 Put the apples, cider, orange juice and pips, cinnamon, cloves and water in a large pan. Bring to the boil, cover and simmer for 1 hour.

2 Leave to cool slightly, then pour the fruit into a scalded jelly bag suspended over a non-metallic bowl and leave to drain overnight.

3 Measure the strained fruit juice into a preserving pan. Add 450g/1lb/2¼ cups warmed sugar for every 600ml/1 pint/2½ cups juice.

4 Gently heat the fruit mixture, stirring continuously, over a low heat until all the sugar has completely dissolved.

5 Increase the heat and then boil, without stirring, for a further 10 minutes, or until the jelly reaches setting point (105°C/220°F).

6 Remove the pan from the heat and skim off any scum from the surface of the jelly using a slotted spoon. Ladle the jelly into warmed sterilized jars, then cover, seal and label when cold.

Nutritional information per quantity:
Energy 3975kcal/16,950kJ; Protein 5.4g; Carbohydrate 990.6g, of which sugars 990.6g; Fat 0.3g, of which saturates 0g; Cholesterol 0mg; Calcium 561mg; Fibre 4.8g; Sodium 123mg.

Pomegranate and grenadine jelly

The slightly tart flavoured, jewel-like flesh of the pomegranate makes the most wonderful jelly. Be careful though, because pomegranate juice can stain indelibly when spilt on clothing.

MAKES ABOUT 900G/2LB

6 ripe red pomegranates, peeled,
    and seeds removed from membranes
120ml/4fl oz/$^1/_2$ cup grenadine syrup
juice and pips (seeds) of 2 oranges
300ml/$^1/_2$ pint/1$^1/_4$ cups water
about 900g/2lb/4$^1/_2$ cups
    preserving or granulated (white)
    sugar, warmed

1 Put the pomegranate seeds in a bowl, crush to release their juice.

2 Transfer the pomegramate seeds to a pan and add the grenadine, orange juice and pips, and water.

3 Bring the mixture to the boil, cover and simmer for 1$^1/_2$ hours. Mash the fruit and leave to cool slightly, then pour into a scalded jelly bag suspended over a bowl and leave to drain overnight.

4 Measure the juice into a pan and add 450g/1lb/2$^1/_4$ cups sugar for every 600ml/1 pint/2$^1/_2$ cups juice.

5 Heat the mixture, stirring, over a low heat until all the sugar has dissolved. Increase the heat and boil rapidly, without stirring, for a further 5–10 minutes, or until the jelly reaches setting point (105°C/220°F).

6 Remove the pan from the heat and then skim off any scum from the surface of the jelly using a slotted spoon. Ladle into warmed sterilized jars, cover, seal and label. Store in a cool, dark place.

Nutritional information per quantity:
Energy 3776kcal/16,114kJ; Protein 5.5g; Carbohydrate 1000.5g, of which sugars 1000.5g; Fat 0.2g, of which saturates 0g; Cholesterol 0mg; Calcium 511mg; Fibre 0.8g; Sodium 76mg.

Blackberry and sloe gin jelly

Although they have a wonderful flavour, blackberries are full of pips, so turning them into a deep-coloured jelly is a good way to make the most of this full-flavoured hedgerow harvest. This preserve is delicious served with richly flavoured roast meats such as lamb.

MAKES ABOUT 1.3KG/3LB

450g/1lb sloes (black plums)
600ml/1 pint/2¹/₂ cups cold water
1.8kg/4lb/16 cups blackberries
juice of 1 lemon

about 900g/2lb/4¹/₂ cups preserving
or granulated (white)sugar
45ml/3 tbsp gin

1 Wash the sloes and prick with a fine skewer. Put them in a large heavy pan with the water and bring to the boil. Reduce the heat, cover and simmer for 5 minutes.

2 Briefly rinse the blackberries in cold water and add them to the pan with the lemon juice.

3 Bring the fruit mixture back to a simmer and cook gently, stirring once or twice, for about 20 minutes, or until the sloes are tender and the blackberries are very soft.

4 Pour the fruit and juices into a sterilized jelly bag suspended over a large non-metallic bowl. Leave to drain for at least 4 hours or overnight, until the juices have stopped dripping.

5 Measure the fruit juice into the cleaned preserving pan, adding 450g/1lb/2¹/₄ cups sugar for every 600ml/1 pint/2¹/₂ cups juice.

6 Heat the mixture gently, stirring occasionally, until the sugar has dissolved completely. Bring to the boil, then boil rapidly for about 10 minutes until the jelly reaches setting point (105°C/220°F). Remove the pan from the heat. Skim off any scum from the surface of the jelly using a slotted spoon, then stir in the gin.

7 Pour the jelly into warmed sterilized jars, cover and seal. Store in a cool, dark place and use within 1 year. Once opened, keep the jelly in the refrigerator and eat within 3 months.

Nutritional information per quantity: Energy 3750kcal/15,985kJ; Protein 10.8g; Carbohydrate 984.3g, of which sugars 984.3g; Fat 1.4g, of which saturates 0g; Cholesterol 0mg; Calcium 743mg; Fibre 21g; Sodium 69mg.

Pear and pomegranate jelly

This delicate jelly has a faintly exotic perfume. Pears are not naturally rich in pectin so liquid pectin needs to be added to the jelly during cooking to help it achieve a good set.

MAKES ABOUT 1.2KG/2½LB

900g/2lb pears
pared rind and juice of 2 lemons
1 cinnamon stick
750ml/1¼ pints/3 cups water
900g/2lb red pomegranates
about 900g/2lb/4½ cups preserving or
    granulated (white) sugar
250ml/8fl oz/1 cup liquid pectin
15ml/1 tbsp rose water (optional)

1 Wash and remove the stalks from the pears and chop the fruit roughly. Put the fruit in a large, heavy pan with the lemon rind and juice, cinnamon stick and water.

2 Bring to the boil, reduce the heat, cover and simmer gently for about 15 minutes. Stir, then simmer, uncovered, for a further 15 minutes.

3 While the pears are simmering, cut the pomegranates in half, horizontally, and use a lemon squeezer to extract the juice: there should be about 250ml/8fl oz/1 cup.

4 Add the pomegranate juice to the pan and bring back to the boil. Reduce the heat and simmer for 2 minutes.

5 Pour the fruit and juices into a sterilized jelly bag suspended over a large non-metallic bowl and leave to drip for at least 3 hours.

6 Measure the strained juice into a pan, adding 450g/1lb/2¼ cups sugar for every 600ml/1 pint/ 2½ cups juice. Heat gently, stirring occasionally, until the sugar has dissolved. Bring to the boil, then boil rapidly for 3 minutes. Remove from the heat and stir in the pectin.

7 Skim any scum from the surface of the jelly, then stir in the rose water if using. Pour into warmed sterilized jars. Cover the jars, then seal and label them. Store in a cool, dark place and use within 18 months.

Nutritional information per quantity:
Energy 3756kcal/16,022kJ; Protein 6g; Carbohydrate 993.6g, of which sugars 993.6g; Fat 0.4g, of which saturates 0g; Cholesterol 0mg; Calcium 529mg; Fibre 7.7g; Sodium 66mg.

Bitter lime and juniper jelly

In this sharp, aromatic jelly the distinctive taste of zesty lime and the rich, resinous flavour of juniper berries are enhanced with a hint of aniseed from the splash of Pernod.

MAKES ABOUT 1.6KG/3½LB

6 limes
1.3kg/3lb tart cooking apples
6 juniper berries, crushed
1.75 litres/3 pints/7½ cups water
about 800g/1¾lb/4 cups preserving
    or granulated (white) sugar
45ml/3 tbsp Pernod (optional)

1 Wash the limes and apples thoroughly, then cut them into small pieces. Put the fruit in a large heavy pan together with the juniper berries.

2 Pour over the water, then bring to the boil and simmer for about 1 hour, or until the fruit is very tender and pulpy.

3 Pour the fruit and juices into a sterilized jelly bag suspended over a large bowl. Leave to drain for at least 3 hours, until the juices stop dripping.

4 Measure the juice into a pan, adding 450g/1lb/2¼ cups sugar for every 600ml/1 pint/2½ cups juice. Heat gently, stirring occasionally, until the sugar has dissolved.

5 Increase the heat and bring the to the boil. Continue to boil rapidly for 10 minutes until the jelly reaches setting point (105°C/220°F), then remove the pan from the heat.

6 Skim any scum from the surface of the jelly using a slotted spoon, then stir in the Pernod if using.

7 Pour the jelly carefully into warmed sterilized jars, then cover, seal and label the jars immediately.

8 Store the jelly in a cool, dark place and use within 1 year. Once opened, store the jelly in the refrigerator and eat it within 3 months.

Nutritional information per quantity: Energy 3152kcal/13,448kJ; Protein 4g; Carbohydrate 836g, of which sugars 836g; Fat 0g, of which saturates 0g; Cholesterol 0mg; Calcium 424mg; Fibre 0g; Sodium 48mg.

Cranberry and claret jelly

The slight sharpness of cranberries makes this a superb jelly for serving with rich meats such as lamb or game. Together with claret, the cranberries give the jelly a beautiful deep red colour.

MAKES ABOUT 1.2KG/2½LB

900g/2lb/8 cups fresh or
   frozen cranberries (washed if fresh)
350ml/12fl oz/1½ cups water
about 900g/2lb/4½ cups preserving
   or granulated (white) sugar
250ml/8fl oz/1 cup claret

1 Put the cranberries in a large heavy pan, add the water, cover and bring to the boil. Reduce the heat and simmer for 20 minutes, or until the cranberries are soft.

2 Pour the fruit and juices into a sterilized jelly bag suspended over a bowl. Leave to drain for at least 3 hours, until the juices stop dripping.

3 Measure the drained juice and the claret into a pan, adding 400g/14oz/2 cups sugar for every 600ml/1 pint/2½ cups liquid. Heat gently, stirring occasionally, until all the preserving sugar has dissolved, then bring to the boil and continue to boil rapidly for about 10 minutes, or until the jelly reaches setting point (105°C/220°F).

4 Remove the pan from the heat, then skim off any scum from the surface of the cranberry mixture using a slotted spoon.

5 Carefully pour the cranberry jelly into warmed sterilized jars. Cover the jars, then seal and label them. Store the jelly in a cool, dark place and use within 2 years. Once opened, you should store the cranberry jelly in the refrigerator and eat it within 3 months.

Nutritional information per quantity:
Energy 3821kcal/16,290kJ; Protein 5.7g; Carbohydrate 967.7g, of which sugars 967.7g; Fat 0.3g, of which saturates 0g; Cholesterol 0mg; Calcium 506mg; Fibre 4.8g; Sodium 78mg.

Guava jelly

Fragrant guava makes an aromatic, pale rust-coloured jelly with a soft set and a slightly sweet-sour flavour that is enhanced by lime juice. Guava jelly goes well with goat's cheese.

MAKES ABOUT 900G/2LB

900g/2lb guavas
juice of 2–3 limes
about 600ml/1 pint/2¹/₂ cups
    cold water
about 500g/1¹/₄lb/2¹/₂ cups preserving
    or granulated (white) sugar

1 Thinly peel and halve the guavas. Scoop out the seeds (pips) from the centre of the fruit and discard them.

2 Place the guavas in a pan with 15ml/1 tbsp lime juice and the water – it should just cover the fruit. Bring to the boil, reduce the heat, cover and simmer for 30 minutes, or until the fruit is tender.

3 Pour the fruit and juices into a sterilized jelly bag suspended over a large non-metallic bowl. Leave to drain for at least 3 hours.

4 Measure the juice into a pan, adding 400g/14oz/2 cups sugar and 15ml/1 tbsp lime juice for every 600ml/1 pint/2¹/₂ cups guava juice.

5 Heat gently, stirring occasionally, until the sugar has dissolved, then bring to the boil and boil rapidly for about 10 minutes.

6 When the jelly reaches setting point (105°C/ 220°F), remove from the heat.

7 Skim any scum from the surface of the jelly using a slotted spoon, then pour into warmed sterilized jars. Cover and seal.

8 Store in a cool, dark place and use within 1 year. Once opened, keep refrigerated and eat within 3 months.

Nutritional information per quantity:
Energy 2090kcal/ 8912kJ; Protein 3.4g; Carbohydrate 552.5g, of which sugars 552.5g; Fat 0.3g, of which saturates 0g; Cholesterol 0mg; Calcium 298mg; Fibre 6.6g; Sodium 39mg.

Minted gooseberry jelly

This classic, tart jelly is an ideal complement to roast lamb. It takes on a pinkish tinge during cooking, not green as one would expect.

MAKES ABOUT 1.2KG/2½LB

1.3kg/3lb/12 cups gooseberries
1 bunch fresh mint
750ml/1¼ pints/3 cups cold water
400ml/14fl oz/1²⁄₃ cups white wine vinegar
about 900g/2lb/4½ cups preserving or
   granulated (white) sugar
45ml/3 tbsp chopped fresh mint

1 Place the gooseberries, mint and water in a preserving pan. Bring to the boil, reduce the heat, cover and simmer for 30 minutes, until the gooseberries are soft. Add the vinegar and simmer, uncovered, for a further 10 minutes.

2 Pour the fruit and juices into a sterilized jelly bag suspended over a large bowl. Leave to drain for at least 3 hours, or until the juices stop dripping, then measure the strained juices back into the cleaned preserving pan.

3 Add 450g/1lb/2¼ cups sugar for every 600ml/1 pint/ 2½ cups juice, then heat gently, stirring, until dissolved. Bring to the boil. Cook for 15 minutes to setting point (105°C/220°F). Remove from the heat and skim off any scum. Cool until a thin skin forms, then stir in the mint.

4 Pour the jelly into warmed sterilized jars, cover and seal. Store and use within 1 year. Once opened, store in the refrigerator and eat within 3 months.

Nutritional information per quantity: Energy 3641kcal/15,534kJ; Protein 10g; Carbohydrate 955.5g, of which sugars 955.5g; Fat 2g, of which saturates 0g; Cholesterol 0mg; Calcium 617mg; Fibre 12g; Sodium 64mg.

Dark plum and apple jelly

Use dark-red cooking plums, damsons or wild plums to offset the sweetness of this deep-coloured jelly.

MAKES ABOUT 1.3KG/3LB

900g/2lb plums
450g/1lb tart cooking apples
150ml/¼ pint/²⁄₃ cup cider vinegar
750ml/1¼ pints/3 cups water
about 675g/1½lb/scant 3½ cups
   preserving or granulated (white) sugar

1 Cut the plums in half along the crease, twist the halves apart, then remove the stones (pits) and roughly chop the flesh. Chop the apples, including the cores and skins. Put the fruit in a large heavy pan with the vinegar and water. Bring to the boil, reduce the heat, cover and simmer for 30 minutes or until the fruit is soft and pulpy.

2 Pour the fruit and juices into a sterilized jelly bag suspended over a large bowl. Leave to drain for 3 hours, or until the fruit juices stop dripping.

3 Measure the juice into the cleaned pan, adding 450g/ 1lb/2¼ cups sugar for every 600ml/1 pint/2½ cups juice. Bring the mixture to the boil, stirring occasionally, until the sugar has dissolved. Continue to boil rapidly for 10 minutes, or to setting point (105°C/220°F).

4 Remove the pan from the heat, skim off any scum, then pour into warmed sterilized jars. Cover and seal while hot. Store in a cool, dark place. Use within 1 year.

Nutritional information per quantity: Energy 2803kcal/11,963kJ; Protein 5.5g; Carbohydrate 740.7g, of which sugars 740.7g; Fat 0.4g, of which saturates 0g; Cholesterol 0mg; Calcium 401mg; Fibre 6.4g; Sodium 49mg.

Jams and conserves

Preserving fruits in jams and conserves is one of the best ways of enjoying their delicious flavour all year round. Sweet juicy summer berries and autumn stone and hedgerow fruits can be made into irresistible jams that can be enjoyed at any time of day. All the recipes in this chapter will keep for at least 6 months.

Blueberry and lime jam

The subtle yet fragrant flavour of blueberries can be elusive on its own. Adding a generous quantity of tangy lime juice enhances the flavour and gives this jam a wonderful zesty taste.

MAKES ABOUT 1.3KG/3LB

1.3kg/3lb/12 cups blueberries
finely pared rind and juice of 4 limes
1kg/2¼ lb/5 cups preserving sugar
    with pectin

1 Put the blueberries, lime juice and half the sugar in a large, non-metallic bowl and lightly crush the berries using a potato masher. Set aside for about 4 hours.

2 Tip the crushed berry mixture into a pan and stir in the finely pared lime rind and the remaining preserving sugar. Heat the mixture slowly, stirring continuously, until the preserving sugar has completely dissolved.

3 Increase the heat and bring to the boil. Boil rapidly for about 4 minutes, or until the jam reaches setting point (105°C/220°F).

4 Remove the pan from the heat and set aside for 5 minutes. Stir the jam gently, then pour into warmed sterilized jars. Seal the jars, then label when completely cold. Store in a cool, dark place.

Nutritional information per quantity: Energy 4265kcal/18,162kJ; Protein 16.7g; Carbohydrate 1111.3g, of which sugars 1111.3g; Fat 2.6g, of which saturates 0g; Cholesterol 0mg; Calcium 1063mg; Fibre 40.3g; Sodium 86mg.

Seedless raspberry and passion fruit jam

The pips in raspberry jam can often put people off this wonderful preserve. This version has none of the pips and all of the flavour, and is enhanced by the tangy addition of passion fruit.

MAKES ABOUT 1.3KG/3LB

1.6kg/3¹/₂lb/14 cups raspberries
4 passion fruit, halved
1.3kg/3lb/6¹/₂ cups preserving sugar
    with pectin, warmed
juice of 1 lemon

1 Place the raspberries in a large pan, then scoop out the passion fruit seeds and pulp and add to the raspberries. Cover and cook over a low heat for 20 minutes, or until the juices begin to run.

2 Remove from the heat and leave to cool slightly, then, using the back of a spoon, press the fruit through a coarse sieve (strainer) into a preserving pan.

3 Add the sugar and lemon juice and stir over a low heat until the sugar has dissolved. Bring to the boil and cook for 4 minutes, or until the jam reaches setting point (105°C/220°F).

4 Remove the pan from the heat and skim off any scum. Leave to cool slightly, then pour into warmed sterilized jars. Seal and label, then store in a cool place.

Nutritional information per quantity: Energy 5544kcal/23,688kJ; Protein 30.5g; Carbohydrate 1435.6g, of which sugars 1435.6g; Fat 5g, of which saturates 1.7g; Cholesterol 0mg; Calcium 1096mg; Fibre 42g; Sodium 137mg.

Blackcurrant jam

This jam has a rich, fruity flavour and a wonderfully strong dark colour. It is punchy and delicious with scones for tea or spread on croissants for a continental-style breakfast.

MAKES ABOUT 1.3KG/3LB

1.3kg/3lb/12 cups blackcurrants
grated rind and juice of 1 orange
475ml/16fl oz/2 cups water
1.3kg/3lb/6$\frac{1}{2}$ cups sugar, warmed
30ml/2 tbsp cassis (optional)

1 Place the blackcurrants, orange rind and juice, and water in a large heavy pan. Bring to the boil, reduce the heat and simmer for 30 minutes.

2 Add the warmed sugar to the pan and stir over a low heat until the sugar has dissolved.

3 Bring the mixture to the boil and cook for about 8 minutes, or to setting point (105°C/220°F).

4 Remove the pan from the heat and skim off any scum from the surface of the jam using a slotted spoon. Leave the jam to cool for 5 minutes, then stir in the cassis if using.

5 Carefully pour the jam into warmed sterilized jars and seal. Leave the jars to cool completely, then label and store them in a cool, dark place.

Nutritional information per quantity: Energy 5504kcal/23,503kJ; Protein 18.4g; Carbohydrate 1448.7g, of which sugars 1448.7g; Fat 0.1g, of which saturates 0g; Cholesterol 0mg; Calcium 1474mg; Fibre 46.9g; Sodium 122mg.

Melon and star anise jam

The delicate flavour of melon is brought out by spicy ginger and perfectly complemented by aromatic star anise. Once opened, store this delicious jam in the refrigerator.

MAKES ABOUT 1.3KG/3LB

2 Charentais or cantaloupe melons
450g/1lb/2¼ cups sugar
2 star anise
4 pieces preserved stem ginger in syrup,
    drained and finely chopped
finely grated rind and juice of 2 lemons

1 Peel and seed the melons, then cut into small cubes and layer with the granulated sugar in a large non-metallic bowl. Cover with clear film (plastic wrap) and leave overnight, or until the melons release their juices.

2 Tip the melon and sugar mixture into a large pan and add the star anise, chopped ginger, and the lemon rind and juice. Stir to combine.

3 Bring the mixture to the boil, then lower the heat. Simmer gently for 25 minutes, or until the melon has become transparent and the setting point is reached (105°C/220°F).

4 Spoon the jam into hot sterilized jars and seal. Leave to cool, then label and store in a cool, dark place.

Nutritional information per quantity: Energy 2133kcal/9095kJ; Protein 9.8g; Carbohydrate 554.2g, of which sugars 554.2g; Fat 1.5g, of which saturates 0g; Cholesterol 0mg; Calcium 434mg; Fibre 6g; Sodium 492mg.

Rhubarb and ginger jam

Late summer is the time to make this preserve, when rhubarb leaves are enormous and the stalks thick and green. It has a wonderfully tart, tangy flavour and is delicious spooned over plain cake.

MAKES ABOUT 2KG/4½LB

1kg/2¼lb rhubarb

1kg/2¼lb/5 cups preserving
   or granulated (white) sugar

25g/1oz fresh root ginger, bruised

115g/4oz crystallized ginger

50g/2oz/¼ cup crystallized orange peel,
   chopped

1 Cut the rhubarb into short pieces and layer with the sugar in a glass bowl. Leave to stand overnight.

2 The next day, scrape the rhubarb and sugar mixture into a large, heavy preserving pan.

3 Tie the bruised ginger root in a piece of muslin (cheesecloth) and add it to the rhubarb. Cook gently for 30 minutes, or until the rhubarb has softened.

4 Remove the root ginger from the pan and then stir in the crystallized ginger and orange peel.

5 Bring the mixture to the boil, then cook over a high heat until setting point is reached (105°C/220°F). Leave to cool for a few minutes, then pour into warmed sterilized jars and seal. When completely cool, label and store.

Nutritional information per quantity: Energy 4135kcal/17,664kJ; Protein 14.8g; Carbohydrate 1083.8g, of which sugars 1083.8g; Fat 1.7g, of which saturates 0g; Cholesterol 0mg; Calcium 1582mg; Fibre 17.9g; Sodium 314mg.

Gooseberry jam

Pale green gooseberries and fragrant elderflowers make perfect partners in this aromatic, sharply flavoured jam. Surprisingly, the jam turns pink during cooking.

MAKES ABOUT 2KG/4½LB

1.3kg/3lb/12 cups firm gooseberries,
    topped and tailed
300ml/½ pint/1¼ cups water
1.3kg/3lb/6½ cups sugar, warmed
juice of 1 lemon
2 handfuls of elderflowers removed
    from their stalks

1 Put the gooseberries into a large preserving pan, add the water and bring the mixture to the boil.

2 Cover the pan with a lid and then simmer gently for 20 minutes until the fruit is soft. Using a potato masher, gently mash the fruit to crush it lightly.

3 Add the sugar, lemon juice and elderflowers to the pan and stir over a low heat until the sugar has dissolved. Boil for 10 minutes, or to setting point (105°C/220°F). Remove from the heat, skim off any scum and cool for 5 minutes, then stir. Pot and seal, then leave to cool before labelling.

Nutritional information per quantity: Energy 5369kcal/22,906kJ; Protein 20.8g; Carbohydrate 1397.5g, of which sugars 1397.5g; Fat 5.2g, of which saturates 0g; Cholesterol 0mg; Calcium 1053mg; Fibre 31.2g; Sodium 104mg.

Damson jam

Dark, plump damsons produce a deeply coloured and richly flavoured jam that makes a delicious treat spread on toasted English muffins or warm crumpets at tea time.

MAKES ABOUT 2KG/4½LB

1kg/2¼lb damsons or wild plums
1.4 litres/2¼ pints/6 cups water
1kg/2¼lb/5 cups preserving
    or granulated (white) sugar, warmed

1 Put the damsons in a preserving pan and pour in the water. Bring the fruit mixture to the boil, then reduce the heat and simmer gently until the damsons are soft. Stir in the sugar.

2 Bring the mixture to the boil, skimming off stones (pits) as they rise. Boil until the mixture reaches setting point (105°C/220°F). Leave to cool for 10 minutes, then pot. Seal, then label and store when cool.

COOK'S TIP
It is important to seal the jars as soon as you have filled them to ensure the jam remains sterile. However, you should then leave the jars to cool completely before labelling and storing them to avoid the risk of burns.

Nutritional information per quantity: Energy 4320kcal/18,430kJ; Protein 10g; Carbohydrate 1141g, of which sugars 1141g; Fat 0g, of which saturates 0g; Cholesterol 0mg; Calcium 770mg; Fibre 18g; Sodium 80mg.

Dried apricot jam

This richly flavoured jam can be made at any time of year, so even if you miss the short apricot season, you can still enjoy the delicious taste of sweet, tangy apricot jam all year round.

MAKES ABOUT 2KG/4½LB

675g/1½lb dried apricots
900ml/1½ pints/3¾ cups apple juice
juice and grated rind of 2 unwaxed
    lemons
675g/1½lb/scant 3½ cups preserving
    or granulated (white) sugar, warmed
50g/2oz/½ cup blanched almonds,
    coarsely chopped

1 Put the apricots in a bowl, pour over the apple juice and leave to soak overnight.

2 Transfer the apricots and juice to a preserving pan. Add the lemon juice and rind. Bring to the boil, lower the heat and simmer for 15–20 minutes until the apricots are soft.

3 Add the warmed sugar to the pan and bring to the boil, stirring, until completely dissolved. Boil for 15–20 minutes, or until setting point is reached (105°C/220°F).

4 Stir the chopped blanched almonds into the jam and then leave the mixture to stand for about 15 minutes. Pour the jam into warmed sterilized jars. Seal, then leave to cool completely before labelling. Store in a cool, dark place.

COOK'S TIP
Use the best-quality traditional dried apricots to make this jam. They have a more suitable texture than the soft ready-to-eat dried apricots and will produce a better end result.

Nutritional information per quantity: Energy 4032kcal/17,163kJ; Protein 40.9g; Carbohydrate 955.2g, of which sugars 953.8g; Fat 31.9g, of which saturates 2.2g; Cholesterol 0mg; Calcium 970mg; Fibre 46.2g; Sodium 142mg.

Summer berry and juniper jam

In late summer, there is a moment when all the different varieties of berries suddenly seem to be ripe at the same time. Blending them with juniperin a jam produces a taste reminiscent of gin.

MAKES ABOUT 1.3KG/3LB

675g/1¹/₂lb/6 cups raspberries
675g/1¹/₂lb/6 cups blackberries
10ml/2 tsp juniper berries, crushed
300ml/¹/₂ pint/1¹/₄ cups water
1.3kg/3lb/6¹/₂ cups sugar, warmed
juice of 2 lemons

1 Put the raspberries, blackberries and juniper berries in a large heavy pan with the water. Set the pan over a low heat, then cover and cook gently for about 15 minutes, or until the juices begin to run.

2 Add the sugar and lemon juice to the pan and cook over a low heat, stirring frequently, until the sugar has dissolved (be careful not to break up the berries too much).

3 Bring to the boil and cook for 5–10 minutes, or until the jam reaches setting point (105°C/220°F). Remove the pan from the heat and skim off any scum from the surface using a slotted spoon.

4 Leave the jam to cool for 5 minutes, then stir gently and pour into warmed sterilized jars. Seal and label, then store in a cool, dark place.

Nutritional information per quantity: Energy 5460kcal/23,325kJ; Protein 25.4g; Carbohydrate 1420.6g, of which sugars 1420.6g; Fat 4.1g, of which saturates 1.4g; Cholesterol 0mg; Calcium 1027mg; Fibre 33.8g; Sodium 119mg.

Greengage and almond jam

This is the perfect preserve to make when greengages are readily available in shops, or if you find you have a glut of the fruit. It has a gloriously rich, golden honey colour and a smooth texture that contrasts wonderfully with the little slivers of almond.

MAKES ABOUT 1.3KG/3LB

1.3kg/3lb greengages, stoned (pitted)
350ml/12fl oz/1¹/₂ cups water
juice of 1 lemon
50g/2oz/¹/₂ cup blanched almonds,
    cut into thin slivers
1.3kg/3lb/6¹/₂ cups sugar, warmed

1 Put the greengages and water in a preserving pan with the lemon juice and almond slivers. Bring to the boil, then cover and simmer for 15–20 minutes, or until the greengages are really soft.

2 Add the sugar to the pan and stir over a low heat until the sugar has dissolved. Bring to the boil and cook for 10–15 minutes, or until the jam reaches setting point (105°C/220°F).

3 Remove the pan from the heat and skim off any scum from the surface using a slotted spoon.

4 Leave to cool for 10 minutes, then stir gently and pour into warmed sterilized jars. Seal, then leave to cool completely before labelling. Store in a cool place.

Nutritional information per quantity: Energy 5896kcal/25,135kJ; Protein 24.9g; Carbohydrate 1476.3g, of which sugars 1475g; Fat 29.2g, of which saturates 2.2g; Cholesterol 0mg; Calcium 978mg; Fibre 24.5g; Sodium 111mg.

Cherry-berry conserve

Tart cranberries enliven the taste of cherries and also add an essential dose of pectin to this pretty conserve, which is fabulous spread on crumpets or toast. It is also delicious stirred into meaty gravies and sauces served with roast duck, poultry or pork.

MAKES ABOUT 1.3KG/3LB

350g/12oz/3 cups fresh cranberries,
   coarsely chopped in a food processor
1kg/2¼lb/5½ cups cherries, stoned
   (pitted)
120ml/4fl oz/½ cup blackcurrant
   or raspberry syrup
juice of 2 lemons
250ml/8fl oz/1 cup water
1.3kg/3lb/6½ cups preserving
   or granulated (white) sugar, warmed

1 Put the cranberries, cherries, fruit syrup and lemon juice into a pan. Cover and bring to the boil. Simmer for 20–30 minutes, or until the fruit is very tender.

2 Add the sugar to the pan and heat gently, stirring, until the sugar has dissolved completely.

3 Bring to the boil, then cook for 10 minutes, or to setting point (105°C/220°F). Remove the pan from the heat.

4 Skim off any scum using a slotted spoon and cool for 10 minutes. Stir gently and pour into warmed sterilized jars. Seal, label and store.

Nutritional information per quantity: Energy 5859kcal/24,986kJ; Protein 16.7g; Carbohydrate 1540.4g, of which sugars 1540.4g; Fat 1.4g, of which saturates 0g; Cholesterol 0mg; Calcium 844mg; Fibre 14.6g; Sodium 105mg.

Wild strawberry and rose petal conserve

This fragrant jam is ideal served with cream teas. Rose water complements the strawberries beautifully, but add only a few drops because the flavour can easily become overpowering.

MAKES ABOUT 900G/2LB

900g/2lb/8 cups wild Alpine
    strawberries
450g/1lb/4 cups strawberries, hulled
    and mashed

2 dark-pink rose buds, petals only
juice of 2 lemons
1.3kg/3lb/6½ cups sugar, warmed
a few drops of rose water

1 Put all the strawberries in a non-metallic bowl with the rose petals, lemon juice and warmed sugar. Cover and leave overnight.

2 The next day, transfer the fruit into a large pan and heat gently, stirring, until the sugar has completely dissolved. Boil for 10–15 minutes, or to setting point (105°C/220°F).

3 Stir the rose water into the jam, then remove the pan from the heat. Skim off any scum from the surface using a slotted spoon. Cool for 5 minutes. Stir and pour into warmed sterilized jars. Seal and label, then store.

COOK'S TIP

If you are unable to find wild berries, just use ordinary strawberries instead. Leave the smaller berries whole but mash any large ones.

Nutritional information per quantity: Energy 5487kcal/23,379kJ; Protein 17.3g; Carbohydrate 1439.5g, of which sugars 1439.5g; Fat 1.4g, of which saturates 0g; Cholesterol 0mg; Calcium 905mg; Fibre 14.8g; Sodium 159mg.

Curds, butters and cheeses

These luscious preserves capture the flavours of the season. Butters and curds are thick and spreadable, delicious spooned on to toast or griddled cakes. Cheeses are firmer and can be cut into wedges or slices, or set in small moulds. Serve them as an accompaniment to roast meat or as a sweetmeat after a meal.

Lemon curd

This classic tangy, creamy curd is still one of the most popular of all the curds. It is delicious spread thickly over freshly baked white bread or served with American-style pancakes.

MAKES ABOUT 450G/1LB

3 lemons
200g/7oz/1 cup caster (superfine) sugar
115g/4oz/8 tbsp unsalted (sweet)
   butter, diced
2 large (US extra large) eggs
2 large (US extra large) egg yolks

1 Wash the lemons, then finely grate the rind and place in a large heatproof bowl. Using a sharp knife, halve the lemons and squeeze the juice into the bowl.

2 Set over a pan of gently simmering water and add the sugar and butter. Stir until the sugar has dissolved and the butter melted.

3 Put the eggs and yolks in a bowl and beat together with a fork. Pour the eggs through a sieve (strainer) into the lemon mixture, and whisk well until thoroughly combined.

4 Stir the simmering mixture over the heat constantly until the lemon curd thickens and lightly coats the back of a wooden spoon.

5 When the mixture has thickened sufficiently, remove the pan from the heat and carefully pour the curd into small, warmed sterilized jars.

6 Cover the jars, then seal and label them. Store them in a cool, dark place, ideally in the refrigerator, and use within 3 months. (Once opened, store them in the refrigerator.)

Nutritional information per quantity: Energy 1927kcal/8056kJ; Protein 20.7g; Carbohydrate 212.1g, of which sugars 212.1g; Fat 116.8g, of which saturates 66.2g; Cholesterol 1029mg; Calcium 294mg; Fibre 0g; Sodium 871mg.

Grapefruit curd

If you favour tangy and refreshing preserves, this delicious grapefruit curd is definitely one to try.
To get the best texture and flavour when making curd, try to use really fresh free-range eggs.

MAKES ABOUT 675G/1½LB

finely grated rind and juice of 1 grapefruit
115g/4oz/8 tbsp unsalted (sweet)
    butter, diced
200g/7oz/1 cup caster (superfine) sugar
4 large (US extra large) eggs,
    lightly beaten

1 Put the grapefruit rind and juice in a large heatproof bowl with the butter and sugar, and set over a pan of gently simmering water. Heat the mixture, stirring occasionally, until the sugar has dissolved and the butter melted.

2 Add the beaten eggs to the fruit mixture, straining them through a sieve (strainer).

3 Whisk, then stir constantly over the heat until the mixture thickens and lightly coats the back of a wooden spoon.

4 Pour the curd into small, warmed sterilized jars, cover and seal. Label when the jars are cold. Store in a cool, dark place, and then use within 3 months. (Once opened, store the curd in the refrigerator.)

Nutritional information per quantity: Energy 1954kcal/8174kJ; Protein 26.9g; Carbohydrate 213.8g, of which sugars 213.8g; Fat 116.8g, of which saturates 66.1g; Cholesterol 1006mg; Calcium 248mg; Fibre 0g; Sodium 992mg.

Passion fruit curd

The tropical flavour and aroma of passion fruit fills this curd with a gloriously sunny character.
It is perfect spread on toasted English muffins or little American pancakes.

MAKES ABOUT 675G/1½LB

grated rind and juice of 2 lemons
115g/4oz/8 tbsp unsalted (sweet)
　butter, diced
275g/10oz/1⅓ cups caster
　(superfine) sugar

4 passion fruit
4 eggs
2 egg yolks

1 Place the lemon rind and juice in a large heatproof bowl and add the butter and sugar.

2 Halve the passion fruit and use a teaspoon to scoop the seeds into a sieve (strainer) set over the bowl. Press out all the juice and discard the seeds.

3 Place the bowl over a pan of gently simmering water and stir occasionally until all the sugar has dissolved and the butter has melted.

4 Beat the eggs and yolks together and add to the bowl, pouring them through a sieve, then whisk well to combine. Stir constantly until the mixture thickens and lightly coats the back of a spoon.

5 Pour the curd into small, warmed sterilized jars, cover and seal. Store in a cool, dark place, preferably in the refrigerator, and use within 3 months. (Once opened, store in the refrigerator.)

Nutritional Information per quantity: Energy 2377kcal/9961kJ; Protein 34.4g; Carbohydrate 291.5g, of which sugars 291.5g; Fat 128g, of which saturates 69.3g; Cholesterol 1409mg; Calcium 334mg; Fibre 2g; Sodium 1023mg.

Seville orange curd

Using flavoursome Seville oranges gives this curd a real citrus tang. It is perfect for spreading on toast for breakfast and can also be folded into whipped cream and used as a filling for cakes.

MAKES ABOUT 450G/1LB

2 Seville (Temple) oranges
115g/4oz/8 tbsp unsalted (sweet) butter, diced
200g/7oz/1 cup caster (superfine) sugar
2 large (US extra large) eggs
2 large (US extra large) egg yolks

1 Wash the oranges, then finely grate the rind and place in a large heatproof bowl. Halve the oranges and squeeze the juice into the bowl with the rind.

2 Place the bowl over a pan of gently simmering water and add the butter and sugar. Stir until the sugar has completely dissolved and the butter melted.

3 Put the eggs and yolks in a small bowl and lightly whisk, then pour them into the orange mixture through a sieve (strainer). Whisk the eggs and orange mixture together until thoroughly combined.

4 Stir the orange and egg mixture constantly over the heat until the mixture thickens and lightly coats the back of a wooden spoon.

5 Pour the orange curd into small, warmed sterilized jars, cover and seal. Store in a cool, dark place, preferably in the refrigerator.

Nutritional information per quantity: Energy 2024kcal/8471kJ; Protein 23.3g; Carbohydrate 235.2g, of which sugars 235.2g; Fat 116.9g, of which saturates 66.1g; Cholesterol 1029mg; Calcium 371mg; Fibre 5.1g; Sodium 882mg.

Mango and cardamom butter

You need to use really ripe mangoes for this recipe. If the mangoes are not ripe enough, they will need much longer cooking and will not produce such a richly flavoured, citrus butter.

MAKES ABOUT 675G/1½LB

900g/2lb ripe mangoes, peeled
6 green cardamom pods, split
120ml/4fl oz/½ cup freshly squeezed
    lemon juice
120ml/4fl oz/½ cup freshly squeezed
    orange juice
50ml/2fl oz/scant ¼ cup water
675g/1½lb/scant 3½ cups
    sugar, warmed

1 Cut the mango flesh away from the stones (pits) and chop, then place in a pan with the cardamom pods, fruit juices and water. Cover and simmer for 10 minutes. Remove the lid and simmer for a further 25 minutes, or until the mangoes are very soft and there is very little liquid left in the pan.

2 Remove the cardamom pods from the pan and discard. Transfer the mixture to a food processor and blend to a purée. Press through a sieve (strainer) into a bowl.

3 Measure the purée into a pan, adding 275g/10oz/1⅓ cups warmed sugar for every 600ml/1 pint/2½ cups purée. Gently heat, stirring, until the sugar has dissolved. Increase the heat and then boil for 10–20 minutes, stirring, until a thick butter forms that holds its shape when spooned on to a cold plate.

4 Spoon the mango and cardamom butter into warmed sterilized jars. Seal and label, then store in a cool, dark place for at least 2 days before eating.

Nutritional information per quantity: Energy 3216kcal/13,735kJ; Protein 10.3g; Carbohydrate 842.8g, of which sugars 840.1g; Fat 1.9g, of which saturates 0.9g; Cholesterol 0mg; Calcium 478mg; Fibre 23.5g; Sodium 70mg.

Plum butter

Simmering plums down into a butter concentrates their tart, tangy flavour and creates a preserve with a wonderful rich, red colour and a really smooth, luxurious texture.

MAKES ABOUT 900G/2LB

900g/2lb red plums, stoned (pitted)
grated rind and juice of 1 orange
150ml/1/4 pint/2/3 cup water
450g/1lb/21/4 cups sugar, warmed

1 Place the plums in a large, heavy pan with the orange rind and juice and the water. Bring to the boil, then cover with a lid and cook for 20–30 minutes, or until the plums are very soft. Set aside to cool.

2 Press the fruit through a fine sieve (strainer). Measure the purée into a pan and add 350g/12oz/1¾ cups sugar for every 600ml/1 pint/2½ cups purée. Gently heat, stirring.

3 When the sugar has dissolved, increase the heat and boil for 10–15 minutes, stirring frequently, until the mixture holds its shape when spooned on to a cold plate.

4 Spoon the mixture into warmed sterilized jars. Seal and label, then store them in a cool, dark place for 2 days to mature before serving.

COOK'S TIP
You can serve this plum butter on toasted walnut and raisin bread for a delicious breakfast, or as a tea time treat. It is also excellent served as a snack at any time of the day.

Nutritional information per quantity: Energy 2097kcal/8960kJ; Protein 7.7g; Carbohydrate 549.5g, of which sugars 549.5g; Fat 0.9g, of which saturates 0g; Cholesterol 0mg; Calcium 355mg; Fibre 14.4g; Sodium 45mg.

Golden peach butter

There is something quite decadent about this subtle, aromatic butter. Its wonderfully rich, dark golden colour and spicy, fragrant flavour make it a real treat every time.

MAKES ABOUT 2.25KG/5LB

1.3kg/3lb ripe peaches, stoned (pitted) and sliced
600ml/1 pint/2½ cups water
675g/1½lb/scant 3½ cups sugar, warmed
grated rind and juice of 1 lemon
2.5ml/½ tsp ground cinnamon
2.5ml/½ tsp ground nutmeg

1 Put the peaches and water in a large pan. Bring to the boil, then cover and simmer for about 10 minutes. Remove the lid and simmer gently for 45 minutes, or until the peaches are quite soft.

2 Remove from the heat, leave to cool slightly, then transfer to a food processor or blender and process to a purée. Press the purée through a fine sieve (strainer) into a bowl. Measure the purée into a large heavy pan, adding 275g/10oz/1⅓ cups warmed sugar for every 600ml/1 pint/2½ cups of purée.

3 Stir the lemon rind and juice and spices into the pan. Heat gently, stirring, until the sugar has dissolved.

4 Bring the mixture to the boil and then continue to cook for 15–20 minutes, stirring frequently, until the mixture forms a thick purée that holds its shape when spooned on to a cold plate. Spoon the butter into small, warmed sterilized jars. Seal and label, then store in a cool, dark place for 2 days before eating.

Nutritional information per quantity: Energy 3089kcal/13,193kJ; Protein 16.4g; Carbohydrate 804.2g, of which sugars 804.2g; Fat 1.3g, of which saturates 0g; Cholesterol 0mg; Calcium 449mg; Fibre 19.5g; Sodium 54mg.

Pear and vanilla butter

The delicate flavour of pears is enhanced by vanilla in this butter that really captures the essence of the fruit. It is well worth allowing it to mature for a few days before eating.

MAKES ABOUT 675G/1½LB

900g/2lb pears, peeled, cored
   and chopped
juice of 3 lemons
300ml/½ pint/1¼ cups water
1 vanilla pod (bean), split
675g/1½lb/scant 3½ cups
   sugar, warmed

1 Place the pears in a pan with the lemon juice, water and vanilla pod. Bring to the boil, cover and simmer for 10 minutes. Uncover and cook for a further 15–20 minutes, or until the pears are very soft.

2 Remove the vanilla pod from the pan, then scrape the seeds into the mixture using the tip of a knife. Tip the fruit and juices into a food processor or blender and blend to a purée. Press the purée through a fine sieve (strainer) into a bowl.

3 Measure the purée into a large, heavy pan, adding 275g/10oz/ 1⅓ cups of warmed sugar for every 600ml/1 pint/2½ cups of purée. Stir over a low heat until the sugar dissolves, increase the heat and bring to the boil.

4 Boil for 15 minutes, stirring, until the mixture forms a thick purée that holds its shape. Spoon into warmed sterilized jars. Seal, label and store in a cool, dark place for at least 2 days before eating.

Nutritional information per quantity: Energy 3019kcal/12,868kJ; Protein 6.1g; Carbohydrate 795.4g, of which sugars 795.4g; Fat 0.9g, of which saturates 0g; Cholesterol 0mg; Calcium 457mg; Fibre 19.8g; Sodium 68mg.

Pumpkin and maple butter

This all-American butter has a lovely bright, autumnal colour and flavour. It is perfect served spread on little pancakes fresh from the griddle, or used as a filling or topping for cakes.

MAKES ABOUT 675G/1½LB

1.2kg/2½lb pumpkin or butternut
    squash, peeled, seeded and chopped
450ml/¾ pint/scant 2 cups water
grated rind and juice of 1 orange
5ml/1 tsp ground cinnamon
120ml/4fl oz/½ cup maple syrup
675g/1½lb/scant 3½ cups
    sugar, warmed

1 Put the pumpkin or squash in a pan with the water and cook for 40 minutes, or until very tender. Drain and press through a sieve (strainer) into a bowl.

2 Stir the orange rind and juice, cinnamon and maple syrup into the purée, then measure the purée into a large pan, adding 275g/10oz/1⅓ cups warmed sugar for every 600ml/1 pint/2½ cups purée.

3 Gently heat the purée, stirring, until the sugar has dissolved. Increase the heat and bring to the boil, then boil for 10–20 minutes, stirring, until the mixture forms a thick purée that holds its shape when spooned on to a cold plate.

4 Remove from the heat and spoon into small, warmed sterilized jars. Seal and label, then store in a cool, dark place for 2 days before eating.

Nutritional information per quantity: Energy 3191kcal/13,606kJ; Protein 12.4g; Carbohydrate 831g, of which sugars 825g; Fat 2.5g, of which saturates 1.2g; Cholesterol 0mg; Calcium 730mg; Fibre 12g; Sodium 369mg.

Apple and cinnamon butter

Fans of apple pies and crumbles will love this luscious apple butter. Serve it on toast or with warmed brioche for a breakfast treat or with pancakes and cream for tea.

MAKES ABOUT 1.8KG/4LB

475ml/16fl oz/2 cups dry (hard) cider
450g/1lb tart cooking apples, peeled,
  cored and sliced
450g/1lb eating apples, peeled, cored
  and sliced

grated rind and juice of 1 lemon
675g/1¹/₂lb/scant 3¹/₂ cups
  sugar, warmed
5ml/1 tsp ground cinnamon

1 Pour the cider into a large pan and bring to the boil. Continue to boil the cider hard until the volume is reduced by half, then add all the sliced apples and the lemon rind and juice.

2 Cover the pan with a lid and cook for 10 minutes, then remove the lid and continue cooking for about 20–30 minutes, or until all the apples are very soft and tender.

3 Remove the pan from the heat, then leave the mixture to cool slightly. Pour the mixture into a food processor or blender and blend to a purée. Press the purée through a fine sieve (strainer) into a bowl.

4 Measure the purée into a large heavy pan, adding 275g/10oz/1¹/₃ cups warmed sugar for every 600ml/1 pint/2¹/₂ cups of purée. Add the ground cinnamon and stir well to combine.

5 Gently heat the mixture, stirring continuously, until all the sugar has completely dissolved. Increase the heat and then boil steadily for about 20 minutes, stirring frequently, until the mixture forms a thick purée that holds its shape when spooned on to a cold plate.

6 Spoon the apple and cinnamon butter into warmed sterilized jars. Seal and label, then store in a cool, dark place for at least 2 days to allow the flavours to develop before serving.

Nutritional information per quantity: Energy 3145kcal/13,428kJ; Protein 6.1g; Carbohydrate 797.8g, of which sugars 797.8g; Fat 0.9g, of which saturates 0g; Cholesterol 0mg; Calcium 432mg; Fibre 14.4g; Sodium 92mg.

Spiced cherry cheese

*For the best results, try to use cherries that have a good tart flavour and dark red flesh.
Serve as an accompaniment to strong cheese, or sliced with roast duck or pork.*

MAKES ABOUT 900G/2LB

1.5kg/3lb 5oz/8¼ cups cherries,
    stoned (pitted)
2 cinnamon sticks
800g/1¾lb/4 cups sugar, warmed

1 Put the cherries and cinnamon in a pan. Pour in enough water to almost cover the fruit. Bring to the boil, cover and simmer for 30 minutes, or until the cherries are tender. Remove the cinnamon and discard.

2 Tip the fruit into a sieve (strainer) and press into a bowl. Measure into a pan, adding 350g/12oz/1¾ cups warmed sugar for every 600ml/ 1 pint/2½ cups purée.

3 Gently heat the purée, stirring, until the sugar dissolves. Increase the heat and cook for 45 minutes, stirring frequently, until the purée becomes thick enough to form a firm jelly when spooned on to a cold plate.

4 Spoon the thickened cheese into warmed sterilized jars or oiled moulds. Seal and label, and then store them in a cool, dark place.

Nutritional information per quantity: Energy 3872kcal/16,493kJ; Protein 17.5g; Carbohydrate 1008.5g, of which sugars 1008.5g; Fat 1.5g, of which saturates 0g; Cholesterol 0mg; Calcium 619mg; Fibre 13.5g; Sodium 63mg.

Blackberry and apple cheese

This rich, dark preserve has an incredibly intense flavour and fabulous colour. For a fragrant twist, add a few raspberries – or even strawberries – in place of some of the blackberries.

MAKES ABOUT 900G/2LB

900g/2lb/8 cups blackberries
450g/1lb tart cooking apples, cut into
    chunks, with skins and cores intact
grated rind and juice of 1 lemon
800g/1³/₄lb/4 cups sugar, warmed

1 Put the fruit, lemon rind and juice in a pan and pour in enough water to come halfway up the fruit. Bring to the boil, then simmer for 15 minutes or until the fruit is very soft. Leave to cool slightly, then tip into a sieve (strainer) and press into a bowl. Measure the purée into a pan, adding 400g/14oz/2 cups warmed sugar for every 600ml/1 pint/2¹/₂ cups purée.

2 Heat gently, stirring, until the sugar dissolves. Increase the heat and cook for 40–50 minutes, stirring frequently, until thick enough to form a firm jelly when spooned on to a chilled plate.

3 Spoon into warmed sterilized jars. Seal and label the jars, then store in a cool, dark place for 2–3 months to dry out slightly.

Nutritional information per quantity: Energy 3534kcal/15064kJ; Protein 13.5g; Carbohydrate 921.9g, of which sugars 921.9g; Fat 2.3g, of which saturates 0g; Cholesterol 0mg; Calcium 811mg; Fibre 35.1g; Sodium 75mg.

Damson cheese

You can use any type or variety of plum for this cheese, but damsons have the most intense flavour. This cheese is good with roast lamb, duck and game, or semi-soft cheese.

MAKES ABOUT 900G/2LB

1.5kg/3lb 5oz damsons
1 vanilla pod (bean), split
800g/1¾lb/4 cups sugar, warmed

1 Wash the damsons and place in a large pan with the vanilla pod and pour in enough water to come halfway up the fruit. Cover and simmer for 30 minutes.

2 Remove the vanilla pod from the pan and scrape the seeds back into the pan using the point of a knife.

3 Press the fruit and juices through a sieve (strainer) into a bowl. Measure the purée into a large, heavy pan, adding 400g/14oz/2 cups sugar for every 600ml/1 pint/ 2½ cups purée.

4 Gently heat the purée, stirring, until the sugar has dissolved. Increase the heat slightly and cook for about 45 minutes, stirring frequently with a wooden spoon, until very thick.

5 Spoon the damson cheese into warmed sterilized jars. Seal and label, then store in a cool, dark place for 2–3 months to dry out slightly before eating.

Nutritional information per quantity: Energy 3722kcal/15,878kJ; Protein 11.5g; Carbohydrate 980g, of which sugars 980g; Fat 0g, of which saturates 0g; Cholesterol 0mg; Calcium 784mg; Fibre 27g; Sodium 78mg.

Quince cheese

This fragrant fruit cheese is particularly good set in squares, dusted with sugar and served as a sweetmeat, but it is just as good bottled in jars and spooned out as required.

MAKES ABOUT 900G/2LB

1.3kg/3lb quinces
800g/1¾lb/4 cups sugar, warmed
caster (superfine) sugar, for dusting

1 Wash the quinces, then chop and place in a large pan. Pour in enough water to nearly cover the fruit, then cover with a lid and simmer for 45 minutes, or until the fruit is very tender. Cool slightly.

2 Press the mixture through a fine sieve (strainer) into a bowl. Measure the purée into a large, heavy pan, adding 400g/14oz/2 cups sugar for every 600ml/1 pint/ 2½ cups purée. Heat gently, stirring, until the sugar has dissolved. Increase the heat and cook for 40–50 minutes, stirring frequently, until very thick.

3 Pour the mixture into a small oiled baking tin (pan) and leave to set for 24 hours. Cut into small squares, dust with sugar and store in an airtight container.

COOK'S TIP
Rather than setting the cheese and cutting it into squares, simply spoon the mixture into warmed sterilized, straight-sided jars. Seal and label, then store in a cool, dark place for 2–3 months to dry out slightly before eating.

Nutritional information per quantity: Energy 3672kcal/15,645kJ; Protein 7.9g; Carbohydrate 966g, of which sugars 966g; Fat 1.3g, of which saturates 0g; Cholesterol 0mg; Calcium 567mg; Fibre 28.6g; Sodium 87mg.

Sweet fruit preserves

Seasonal fruits bottled in spirits or syrups can look stunning stacked on your shelves and taste divine spooned over ice cream, cakes and desserts. Preserving them in syrups and alcohol helps to retain their colour, texture and flavour, while ensuring that they do not ferment or spoil on keeping.

Kumquats and limequats in brandy syrup

These yellow and green fruits are highly decorative and taste very good indeed, so make a few extra jars of this luxurious preserve to enjoy throughout the coming months.

MAKES ABOUT 900G/2LB

450g/1lb kumquats and limequats
175g/6oz/scant 1 cup sugar
600ml/1 pint/2^1/$_2$ cups water
150ml/^{1}/$_4$ pint/^{2}/$_3$ cup brandy
15ml/1 tbsp orange flower water

1 Using a cocktail stick (toothpick), prick each kumquat and limequat several times.

2 Put the sugar and water in a large pan and heat, stirring, until the sugar has dissolved. Bring to the boil, add the fruit and simmer for 25 minutes, or until tender. Using a slotted spoon, remove the fruit to warmed sterilized jars. The remaining syrup should be fairly thick: if not, boil for a few minutes, then remove from the heat and leave to cool very slightly.

3 Stir the brandy and orange flower water into the syrup, then pour over the fruit and seal immediately. Store in a cool, dark place and use within 6 months.

COOK'S TIP
Kumquats and limequats are unusual among the citrus family because they are eaten whole and do not need to be peeled. Their thin skins have a pleasantly bitter flavour.

Nutritional information per quantity: Energy 1189kcal/5031kJ; Protein 4.9g; Carbohydrate 222g, of which sugars 222g; Fat 0.4g, of which saturates 0g; Cholesterol 0mg; Calcium 232mg; Fibre 5.4g; Sodium 28mg.

Clementines in juniper syrup

Whole clementines preserved in spiced syrup make a lovely dessert served on their own, with a spoonful of mascarpone or clotted cream. They also make an excellent addition to trifles.

MAKES ABOUT 1.3KG/3LB

5cm/2in piece fresh root ginger, sliced
6 whole cloves, plus extra for the jars
5ml/1 tsp juniper berries, crushed, plus extra for the jars
900g/2lb/4^1/$_2$ cups sugar
1.2 litres/2 pints/5 cups water
1.3kg/3lb clementines, peeled

1 Tie the ginger, cloves and juniper berries together in a small muslin (cheesecloth) bag. Put the sugar and water in a large pan and heat gently, stirring, until the sugar has dissolved. Add the spice bag to the pan, bring to the boil and cook for 5 minutes.

2 Add the clementines to the pan and simmer for about 8–10 minutes, or until tender. Using a slotted spoon, remove the fruit from the syrup and drain well.

3 Pack the hot fruit into warmed sterilized jars and add a few cloves and juniper berries to each jar. Pour off any excess liquid.

4 Return the syrup to the boil and then boil rapidly for 10 minutes. Leave the syrup to cool slightly, then pour over the fruit to cover completely. Twist and gently tap the jars to release any trapped air bubbles, then seal and store in a cool, dark place.

Nutritional information per quantity: Energy 4027kcal/17,183kJ; Protein 16.2g; Carbohydrate 1053.6g, of which sugars 1053.6g; Fat 1.3g, of which saturates 0g; Cholesterol 0mg; Calcium 880mg; Fibre 15.6g; Sodium 106mg.

Mulled pears

These pretty pears in a warming spiced syrup make a tempting dessert, particularly during the cold winter months. Serve them with crème fraîche or vanilla ice cream, or in open tarts.

MAKES ABOUT 1.3KG/3LB

1.8kg/4lb small firm pears
1 orange
1 lemon
2 cinnamon sticks, halved
12 whole cloves
5cm/2in piece fresh root ginger,
    peeled and sliced
300g/11oz/1¹/₂ cups sugar
1 bottle fruity light red wine

1 Peel the pears, leaving the stalks intact. Peel very thin strips of rind from the orange and lemon, using a vegetable peeler. Pack the pears and citrus rind into large sterilized preserving jars, dividing the spices evenly between the jars.

2 Preheat the oven to 120°C/250°F/Gas ¹/₂. Put the sugar and wine in a large pan and heat gently, stirring, until the sugar has completely dissolved. Bring the mixture to the boil, then cook for 5 minutes.

3 Pour the wine syrup over the pears, making sure that there are no air pockets and that the fruits are completely covered with the syrup.

4 Cover the jars with their lids, but do not seal. Place them in the oven and cook for 2¹/₂–3 hours.

5 Carefully remove the jars from the oven, place on a dry dish towel and seal. Leave the jars to cool completely, then label and store in a cool, dark place.

Nutritional information per quantity: Energy 2412kcal/10,208kJ; Protein 7.6g; Carbohydrate 495g, of which sugars 495g; Fat 1.8g, of which saturates 0g; Cholesterol 0mg; Calcium 409mg; Fibre 39.6g; Sodium 124mg.

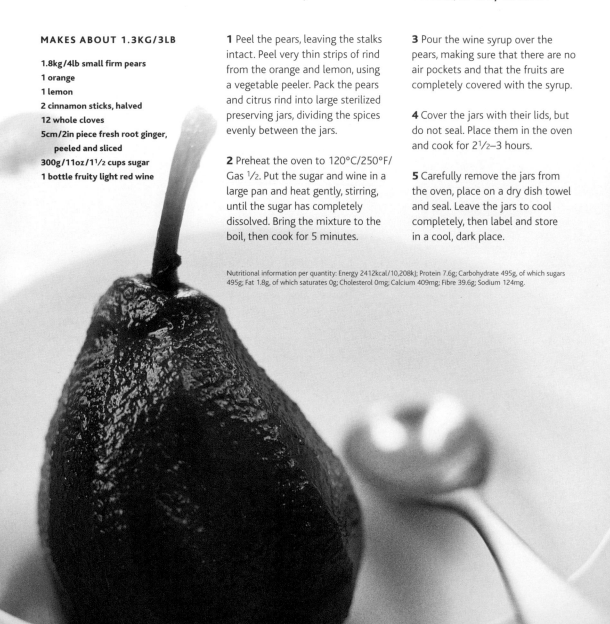

Peaches in peach schnapps

The fragrant taste of peaches is complemented and intensified by the addition of the schnapps. Serve with whipped cream flavoured with some of the syrup and a squeeze of lemon juice.

MAKES ABOUT 1.3KG/3LB

1.3kg/3lb firm peaches
1 litre/1³/₄ pints/4 cups water
900g/2lb/4¹/₂ cups sugar
8 green cardamom pods
50g/2oz/¹/₂ cup whole blanched
    almonds, toasted
120ml/4fl oz/¹/₂ cup peach schnapps

1 Put the peaches in a bowl and pour over boiling water. Drain immediately and peel, then halve and remove the stones (pits). Put the water and half the sugar in a large pan and heat gently until the sugar has dissolved. Increase the heat and boil for 5 minutes.

2 Add the peaches to the syrup and return to the boil. Reduce the heat, cover and simmer gently for 5–10 minutes, or until tender but not too soft. Remove the peaches and set aside to drain.

3 Put the cardamom pods and almonds in a pan, adding 900ml/1¹/₂ pints/3³/₄ cups of the syrup and the remaining sugar. Heat, stirring, until the sugar has dissolved. Bring to the boil and boil until the syrup reaches 104°C/219°F. Leave to cool slightly, remove the cardamom pods, then stir in the schnapps.

4 Pack the peaches loosely in warmed sterilized jars. Pour over the syrup and almonds, tapping the jars to release air bubbles. Seal and store in a cool, dark place for 2 weeks before eating.

Nutritional information per quantity: Energy 4595kcal/19,561kJ; Protein 28.1g; Carbohydrate 1082.1g, of which sugars 1080.8g; Fat 29.2g, of which saturates 2.2g; Cholesterol 0mg; Calcium 694mg; Fibre 23.2g; Sodium 88mg.

Pineapple in coconut rum

The tropical flavour of pineapple is enhanced by the addition of coconut rum. For a really special treat, serve topped with whipped cream and grated bitter chocolate.

MAKES ABOUT 900G/2LB

1 orange
1.2 litres/2 pints/5 cups water
900g/2lb/4¹⁄₂ cups sugar

2 pineapples, peeled, cored and cut
   into small chunks
300ml/¹⁄₂ pint/1¹⁄₄ cups coconut rum

1 Thinly pare strips of rind from the orange, then slice the rind into thin matchsticks. Put the water and half the sugar in a large pan with the orange rind and heat gently until the sugar has dissolved. Increase the heat and boil for 5 minutes.

2 Carefully add the pineapple pieces to the syrup and return to the boil. Reduce the heat and simmer gently for 10 minutes. Using a slotted spoon, remove the pineapple from the pan and set aside to drain.

3 Add the remaining sugar to the syrup and heat, stirring, until dissolved. Bring to the boil, then boil for 10 minutes, or until thickened. Remove from the heat and cool slightly. Stir in the coconut rum.

4 Pack the pineapple loosely in warmed sterilized jars. Pour in the syrup until the fruit is covered, tapping and twisting the jars to release any air bubbles. Seal, label and store in a cool, dark place for 2 weeks before eating.

COOK'S TIP
Choose plump pineapples that feel heavy for their size, with fresh, stiff plumes. To test for ripeness, gently pull out one of the bottom leaves; it should come out easily.

Nutritional information per quantity: Energy 4660kcal/19,834kJ; Protein 7.7g; Carbohydrate 1119.7g, of which sugars 1119.7g; Fat 1.6g, of which saturates 0g; Cholesterol 0mg; Calcium 636mg; Fibre 9.6g; Sodium 106mg.

Forest berries in kirsch

This preserve captures the essence of the season in its rich, dark colour and flavour. Adding the sweet cherry liqueur Kirsch to the syrup intensifies the flavour of the bottled fruit.

MAKES ABOUT 1.3KG/3LB

1.3kg/3lb/12 cups mixed prepared
    summer berries, such as blackberries,
    raspberries, strawberries, redcurrants
    and cherries
225g/8oz/generous 1 cup sugar
600ml/1 pint/2¹/₂ cups water
120ml/4fl oz/¹/₂ cup Kirsch

1 Preheat the oven to 120°C/250°F/Gas ¹/₂. Pack the prepared fruit loosely into sterilized jars. Cover without sealing and place in the oven for 50–60 minutes, or until the juices start to run.

2 Meanwhile, put the sugar and water in a large pan and heat gently, stirring, until the sugar has dissolved. Increase the heat, boil for 5 minutes, then stir in the Kirsch and set aside.

3 Carefully remove the jars from the oven and place them on a dish towel on a heatproof work surface. Use the fruit from one of the jars to top up the rest.

4 Remove the boiling syrup from the heat, then carefully pour it into each jar, twisting and tapping each one to ensure that no air bubbles have been trapped. Seal, then store in a cool, dark place.

Nutritional information per quantity: Energy 1517kcal/6487kJ; Protein 19.3g; Carbohydrate 334.1g, of which sugars 334.1g; Fat 3.9g, of which saturates 1.3g; Cholesterol 0mg; Calcium 444mg; Fibre 32.5g; Sodium 52mg.

Cherries in eau de vie

These potent cherries should be consumed with respect because they pack quite an alcoholic punch. Serve them with rich, dark chocolate torte or as a wicked topping for creamy rice pudding.

MAKES ABOUT 1.3KG/3LB

450g/1lb/generous 3 cups ripe cherries
8 blanched almonds
75g/3oz/6 tbsp sugar
500ml/17fl oz/generous 2 cups
   eau de vie

1 Wash and stone (pit) all of the cherries then pack them into a sterilized, wide-necked bottle along with the blanched almonds. Spoon the sugar into the bottle over the fruit.

2 Pour in the eau de vie to cover all the fruit and seal tightly.

3 Store for at least 1 month before serving, shaking the bottle now and then to help dissolve the sugar.

Nutritional information per quantity:
Energy 1479kcal/6142kJ; Protein 9.3g; Carbohydrate 53.5g, of which sugars 52.8g; Fat 14.4g, of which saturates 1.1g; Cholesterol 0mg; Calcium 119mg; Fibre 5.9g; Sodium 8mg..

Spiced apple mincemeat

This gently spiced mincemeat is traditionally used to fill little pies at Christmas but is great at any time of the year. Use it as a filling for larger tarts with lattice tops and serve with creamy custard. To make it lighter, add some extra grated apple just before using.

MAKES ABOUT 1.8KG/4LB

500g/1¹/₄lb tart cooking apples, peeled, cored and finely diced

115g/4oz/¹/₂ cup ready-to-eat dried apricots, coarsely chopped

900g/2lb/5¹/₃ cups luxury dried mixed fruit

115g/4oz/1 cup whole blanched almonds, chopped

175g/6oz/1 cup shredded beef suet or vegetarian suet (chilled, grated shortening)

225g/8oz/generous 1 cup dark muscovado (molasses) sugar

grated rind and juice of 1 orange

grated rind and juice of 1 lemon

5ml/1 tsp ground cinnamon

2.5ml/¹/₂ tsp grated nutmeg

2.5ml/¹/₂ tsp ground ginger

120ml/4fl oz/¹/₂ cup brandy

1 Put the apples, apricots, dried mixed fruit, almonds, suet and sugar in a large non-metallic bowl and stir together until thoroughly combined.

2 Add the orange and lemon rind and juice, cinnamon, nutmeg, ginger and brandy to the bowl and mix together well. Cover the bowl with a clean dish towel and leave to stand in a cool place for 2 days, stirring occasionally.

3 Spoon the mincemeat into cool sterilized jars, pressing down well, and being very careful not to trap any air bubbles. Cover and seal.

4 Store the jars in a cool, dark place for at least 4 weeks before using. Once opened, store in the refrigerator and use within 4 weeks. Unopened, the mincemeat will keep for 1 year.

Nutritional information per quantity: Energy 6071kcal/25,579kJ; Protein 52.2g; Carbohydrate 963.6g, of which sugars 939.7g; Fat 227.3g, of which saturates 92.4g; Cholesterol 144mg; Calcium 1156mg; Fibre 44.4g; Sodium 488mg.

Figs infused with Earl Grey

The aromatic flavour of Earl Grey tea in this syrup permeates the figs to create a sweet and intriguing flavour. They are delicious spooned over creamy Greek yogurt.

MAKES ABOUT 1.8KG/4LB

900g/2lb ready-to-eat dried figs
1.2 litres/2 pints/5 cups Earl Grey tea
pared rind of 1 orange
1 cinnamon stick
275g/10oz/1¹/₃ cups sugar
250ml/8fl oz/1 cup brandy

1 Put the figs in a pan and add the tea, orange rind and cinnamon stick. Bring to the boil, cover and simmer for 10–15 minutes, or until the figs are tender.

2 Using a slotted spoon, remove the figs from the pan and leave to drain. Add the sugar to the tea and heat gently, stirring, until the sugar has dissolved. Boil rapidly for 2 minutes until syrupy.

3 Remove the pan from the heat, then stir in the brandy. Pack the figs and orange rind into warmed sterilized jars and pour in the hot syrup to cover. Twist and gently tap the jars to expel any air bubbles, then seal and store in a cool, dark place for 1 month.

Nutritional information per quantity: Energy 3519kcal/14,921kJ; Protein 31.1g; Carbohydrate 724.8g, of which sugars 724.8g; Fat 13.5g, of which saturates 0g; Cholesterol 0mg; Calcium 2216mg; Fibre 62.1g; Sodium 530mg.

Apricots in amaretto syrup

Amaretto brings out the delicious flavour of apricots. Try serving the drained fruit on top of a tart filled with crème pâtissière, using some of the amaretto syrup to glaze the apricots.

MAKES ABOUT 900G/2LB

1.3kg/3lb firm apricots
1 litre/1³/4 pints/4 cups water
800g/1³/4lb/4 cups sugar
1 vanilla pod (bean)
175ml/6fl oz/³/4 cup amaretto liqueur

1 Cut a slit in each apricot and remove the stone (pit), keeping the fruit intact. Put the water, half the sugar and the vanilla pod in a large pan. Heat gently, stirring, until the sugar dissolves. Increase the heat and simmer for 5 minutes.

2 Add the apricots to the syrup and bring almost to the boil. Cover and simmer gently for 5 minutes. Remove the apricots with a slotted spoon and drain in a colander.

3 Add the remaining sugar to the pan and heat gently, stirring, until the sugar has dissolved, then boil rapidly until the syrup reaches 104°C/219°F. Cool slightly, then remove the vanilla pod and stir in the amaretto.

4 Pack the apricots loosely in large, warmed sterilized jars. Pour the syrup over, twisting and tapping the jars to expel any air. Seal and store in a cool, dark place for 2 weeks before eating.

Nutritional information per quantity: Energy 3890kcal/16,577kJ; Protein 12.1g; Carbohydrate 958.2g, of which sugars 958.2g; Fat 0.9g, of which saturates 0g; Cholesterol 0mg; Calcium 568mg; Fibre 15.3g; Sodium 87mg.

Blackcurrant brandy

Spoon a little of the brandy into a wine glass and top up with chilled white wine or champagne for a special celebration drink, or serve in small liqueur glasses as a digestif.

MAKES ABOUT 1 LITRE/1¾ PINTS/4 CUPS

900g/2lb/8 cups blackcurrants, washed
600ml/1 pint/2½ cups brandy
350g/12oz/1¾ cups sugar

1 Strip the blackcurrants off their stems and pack the fruit into a sterilized 1.5-litre/2½-pint/6¼-cup preserving jar. Using the back of a wooden spoon, crush the blackcurrants lightly.

2 Add the brandy and sugar to the jar, ensuring the fruit is completely covered by the brandy. Twist and gently tap the jar to ensure there are no trapped air bubbles.

3 Seal the jar, then store in a cool, dark place for about 2 months, shaking the jar occasionally.

4 Pour the liquor through a sieve (strainer) lined with a double layer of muslin (cheesecloth) into a sterilized jug (pitcher). Pour into sterilized bottles, seal, label and store in a cool, dark place.

Nutritional information per quantity: Energy 2963kcal/12,487kJ; Protein 9.8g; Carbohydrate 425.1g, of which sugars 425.1g; Fat 0g, of which saturates 0g; Cholesterol 0mg; Calcium 725mg; Fibre 32.4g; Sodium 48mg.

Blueberries in gin syrup

These aromatic berries preserved in a gin-laced syrup make a wonderful combination. The syrup turns a fabulous blue colour and the gin's flavour complements the blueberries.

MAKES ABOUT 1.8KG/4LB

1.3kg/3lb/12 cups blueberries
225g/8oz/1 cup sugar
600ml/1 pint/2½ cups water
120ml/4fl oz/½ cup gin

1 Preheat the oven to 120°C/250°F/Gas ½. Pack the blueberries into sterilized jars and cover them, without sealing. Put the jars in the oven and then bake for 50–60 minutes until the juices start to run.

2 Meanwhile, put the sugar and water in a pan and heat gently, stirring continuously, until the sugar has dissolved completely. Increase the heat, bring to the boil, then boil for 5 minutes. Stir in the gin.

3 Carefully remove the jars from the oven and place on a dry dish towel on a heatproof surface. Use the fruit from one of the jars to top up the others.

4 Carefully pour the syrup into the jars to cover the fruit completely. Twist and gently tap the jars to ensure that no air bubbles have been trapped. Seal and label the jars, then store them in a cool, dark place until ready to serve.

Nutritional information per quantity: Energy 1478kcal/6237kJ; Protein 12.8g; Carbohydrate 301.4g, of which sugars 301.4g; Fat 2.6g, of which saturates 0g; Cholesterol 0mg; Calcium 652mg; Fibre 40.3g; Sodium 39mg.

Rumtopf

This fruit preserve originated in Germany, where special earthenware rumtopf pots are traditionally filled with fruits as they come into season.

**MAKES ABOUT 3 LITRES/
5 PINTS/12½ CUPS**

900g/2lb fruit, such as strawberries,
    blackberries, blackcurrants,
    redcurrants, peaches, apricots,
    cherries and plums, stems, skins, cores
    and stones (pits) removed
250g/9oz/1¼ cups sugar
1 litre/1¾ pints/4 cups white rum

1 Cut any large fruits into bitesize pieces. Combine all the fruit with the sugar in a large non-metallic bowl, then cover and leave to stand for 30 minutes.

2 Spoon the fruit and juices into a sterilized 3-litre/5¼-pint/12½-cup preserving or earthenware jar and pour in the white rum to cover the fruit.

3 Cover the jar with clear film (plastic wrap), then seal and store in a cool, dark place. As space allows, and as different fruits come into season, add more fruit, sugar and rum in appropriate proportions.

4 When the jar is full, store in a cool, dark place for 2 months. Spoon the fruit over desserts and enjoy the rum in glasses as a liqueur.

Nutritional information per quantity: Energy 3448kcal/14,409kJ; Protein 8.4g; Carbohydrate 315.3g, of which sugars 315.3g; Fat 0.9g, of which saturates 0g; Cholesterol 0mg; Calcium 276mg; Fibre 9.9g; Sodium 69mg.

Poached spiced plums in brandy

Bottling plums in a spicy syrup is a great way to preserve the flavours of autumn and provide a store of instant desserts during the winter months. Serve them with whipped cream.

MAKES ABOUT 900G/2LB

600ml/1 pint/2¹/₂ cups brandy
rind of 1 lemon, peeled in a long strip
350g/12oz/1³/₄ cups caster
**   (superfine) sugar**
1 cinnamon stick
900g/2lb plums

1 Put the brandy, lemon rind, sugar and cinnamon in a large pan and heat gently until the sugar dissolves. Add the plums and poach them for 15 minutes until soft. Remove the fruit and pack in sterilized jars.

2 Boil the syrup rapidly until reduced by a third, then strain over the plums to cover. Seal the jars tightly. Label when cold and store for up to 6 months in a cool, dark place.

Nutritional information per quantity: Energy 3035kcal/12,792kJ; Protein 7.1g; Carbohydrate 444.9g, of which sugars 444.9g; Fat 0.9g, of which saturates 0g; Cholesterol 0mg; Calcium 302mg; Fibre 14.4g; Sodium 39mg.

Pickles and chutneys

Sharp and sweet, warm and mellow, or hot and piquant – pickles are the magical condiments that can transform the simplest meals. Try them with cheeses, and cold and roast meats. Chutneys have wonderfully mellow flavours: pair them with cheeses or cold meats, or spread them thickly in sandwiches.

Pickled red cabbage

This delicately spiced and vibrant-coloured pickle is an old-fashioned favourite to serve with bread and cheese for an informal lunch, or to accompany cold ham, duck or goose.

**MAKES ABOUT
1–1.6KG/2¼–3½LB**

675g/1½lb/6 cups red cabbage,
   shredded
1 large Spanish (Bermuda) onion, sliced
30ml/2 tbsp sea salt
600ml/1 pint/2½ cups red wine vinegar
75g/3oz/6 tbsp light muscovado
   (brown) sugar
15ml/1 tbsp coriander seeds
3 cloves
2.5cm/1in piece fresh root ginger
1 whole star anise
2 bay leaves
4 eating apples

1 Put the cabbage and onion in a bowl with the salt and mix until thoroughly combined. Tip into a colander over a bowl and leave to drain overnight.

2 The next day, rinse the salted vegetables, drain well and pat dry using kitchen paper. Pour the vinegar into a pan, add the sugar, spices and bay leaves and bring to the boil. Remove from the heat and leave to cool.

3 Core and chop the apples, then layer with the cabbage and onions in sterilized preserving jars. Pour over the cooled spiced vinegar. (If you prefer a milder pickle, strain out the spices first.) Seal the jars and store for 1 week before eating. Eat within 2 months. Once opened, store in the refrigerator.

Nutritional information per quantity: Energy 674kcal/2868kJ; Protein 12g; Carbohydrate 161.4g, of which sugars 159.3g; Fat 2g, of which saturates 0g; Cholesterol 0mg; Calcium 405mg; Fibre 23g; Sodium 64mg.

English pickled onions

These powerful pickles are traditionally served with a plate of cold meats and bread and cheese. They should be made with malt vinegar and stored for at least 6 weeks before eating.

MAKES ABOUT 4 JARS

1kg/2¼lb pickling onions, peeled
115g/4oz/½ cup salt
750ml/1¼ pints/3 cups malt vinegar
15ml/1 tbsp sugar
2–3 dried red chillies
5ml/1 tsp brown mustard seeds
15ml/1 tbsp coriander seeds
5ml/1 tsp allspice berries
5ml/1 tsp black peppercorns
5cm/2in piece fresh root ginger, sliced
2–3 blades mace
2–3 fresh bay leaves

1 Place the peeled onions in a bowl and cover with cold water, then drain the water into a large pan. Add the salt and heat slightly to dissolve it, then cool before pouring the brine over the onions. Place a plate inside the top of the bowl and weigh it down slightly so that it all the onions remain submerged in the brine. Leave to stand for 24 hours.

2 Meanwhile, place the vinegar in a pan. Wrap all the remaining ingredients, except the bay leaves, in a piece of muslin (cheesecloth). Bring the to the boil, simmer for 5 minutes, then remove from the heat. Leave to infuse overnight. The next day, drain the onions, rinse and pat dry.

3 Pack them into sterilized 450g/1lb jars. Add some or all of the spice from the vinegar, except the ginger slices. Pour enough of the vinegar over to cover and add the bay leaves. (Store left-over vinegar in a bottle for another batch of pickles.) Seal the jars with non-metallic lids and store in a cool, dark place for at least 6 weeks before eating.

Nutritional information per quantity: Energy 109kcal/454kJ; Protein 3.1g; Carbohydrate 24.5g, of which sugars 18.6g; Fat 0.5g, of which saturates 0g; Cholesterol 0mg; Calcium 67mg; Fibre 3.6g; Sodium 8mg.

Pickled turnips and beetroot

This delicious pickle is a Middle-Eastern speciality. The turnips turn a rich red in their beetroot-spiked brine and look gorgeous stacked on shelves in the kitchen.

MAKES ABOUT 1.6KG/3¹⁄₂LB

1kg/2¹⁄₄lb young turnips
3–4 raw beetroots (beets)
about 45ml/3 tbsp coarse sea salt
about 1.5 litres/2¹⁄₂ pints/6¹⁄₄ cups
    water
juice of 1 lemon

1 Wash the turnips and beetroots, but do not peel them, then cut into slices about 5mm/¹⁄₄in thick. Be careful when preparing the beetroots because their bright red juice can stain clothing.

2 Put the salt and water in a bowl, stir and leave to stand until the salt has completely dissolved.

3 Sprinkle the beetroots with lemon juice and place in the bottom of four 1.2-litre/2-pint sterilized jars. Top with sliced turnip, packing them in very tightly, then pour over the brine, making sure that the vegetables are covered.

4 Seal the jars and leave in a cool place for 7 days before serving.

Nutritional information per quantity: Energy 338kcal/1442kJ; Protein 14.1g; Carbohydrate 69.8g, of which sugars 66g; Fat 3.3g, of which saturates 0g; Cholesterol 0mg; Calcium 541mg; Fibre 29.7g; Sodium 4278mg.

Shallots in balsamic vinegar

These whole shallots, cooked in balsamic vinegar and herbs, are a modern variation on traditional pickled onions, with a much more gentle, smooth flavour.

MAKES 1 LARGE JAR

500g/1¼lb shallots
30ml/2 tbsp muscovado (molasses) sugar
several bay leaves and/or fresh
    thyme sprigs
300ml/½ pint/1¼ cups balsamic
    vinegar

1 Put the unpeeled shallots in a bowl. Pour over boiling water and leave to stand for 2 minutes to loosen the skins. Drain and carefully peel the shallots, leaving them whole.

2 Put the sugar, bay leaves and/or thyme and vinegar in a large heavy pan and bring to the boil.

3 Add the shallots, cover and simmer gently for 40 minutes, or until the shallots are just tender.

4 Transfer the shallots and vinegar mixture to a warmed sterilized jar, packing the shallots down well. Seal and label the jar, then store in a cool, dark place for about 1 month before eating.

Nutritional information per quantity: Energy 298kcal/1254kJ; Protein 6.1g; Carbohydrate 70.9g, of which sugars 59.3g; Fat 1g, of which saturates 0g; Cholesterol 0mg; Calcium 141mg; Fibre 7g; Sodium 17mg.

Hot Thai pickled shallots

Although they may be quite difficult to find and require lengthy preparation, Thai pink shallots look and taste exquisite when served as a condiment with a wide range of South-east Asian meals.

MAKES ABOUT 3 JARS

5–6 fresh red or green bird's eye chillies, whole, or halved and seeded if desired

500g/1¼lb Thai pink shallots, peeled (or ordinary shallots or pickling onions, if unavailable)

2 large garlic cloves, peeled, halved and green shoots removed

600ml/1 pint/2½ cups cider vinegar

45ml/3 tbsp sugar

10ml/2 tsp salt

5cm/2in piece fresh root ginger, sliced

15ml/1 tbsp coriander seeds

2 lemon grass stalks, cut in half lengthways

4 kaffir lime leaves or strips of lime rind

15ml/1 tbsp chopped fresh coriander (cilantro)

1 If you are leaving the chillies whole (they will be hotter), prick them several times with a cocktail stick (toothpick).

2 Bring a pan of water to the boil. Blanch the chillies, shallots and garlic for 1–2 minutes, then drain. Rinse under cold water and leave to drain.

3 To prepare the vinegar, put the cider vinegar, sugar, salt, ginger, coriander seeds, lemon grass, and lime leaves or lime rind in a pan and bring to the boil.

4 Simmer over a low heat for 3–4 minutes. Remove the pan from the heat and set aside to cool. Using a slotted spoon, remove the ginger from the pan and discard. Return the vinegar to the boil, then add the fresh coriander, garlic, shallots and chillies, and cook for about 1 minute.

5 Pack the shallots, spices and aromatics into warmed sterilized jars and pour over the hot vinegar. Cool, then seal. Leave in a dark place for 2 months before eating.

Nutritional information per quantity: Energy 127kcal/536kJ; Protein 2.3g; Carbohydrate 30.4g, of which sugars 26.5g; Fat 0.4g, of which saturates 0g; Cholesterol 0mg; Calcium 52mg; Fibre 2.7g; Sodium 7mg.

Pickled mushrooms with garlic

This method of preserving mushrooms is popular throughout Europe. The pickle is good made with cultivated mushrooms, but it is worth including a couple of sliced ceps for their flavour.

MAKES ABOUT 900G/2LB

500g/1¹/4lb/8 cups mixed mushrooms, such as small ceps, chestnut mushrooms and shiitake

300ml/¹/2 pint/1¹/4 cups white wine vinegar or cider vinegar

15ml/1 tbsp sea salt

5ml/1 tsp caster (superfine) sugar

300ml/¹/2 pint/1¹/4 cups water

4–5 fresh bay leaves

8 large fresh thyme sprigs

15 garlic cloves, peeled and halved, with any green shoots removed

1 small red onion, halved and thinly sliced

2–3 small dried red chillies

5ml/1 tsp coriander seeds, lightly crushed

5ml/1 tsp black peppercorns

a few strips of lemon rind

250–350ml/8–12fl oz/1–1¹/2 cups extra virgin olive oil

1 Trim and wipe all the mushrooms with a clean, damp cloth, and then cut any large ones in half.

2 Put the white wine vinegar or cider vinegar in a large pan with the salt, caster sugar and water and then bring the mixture to the boil. Add the bay leaves, thyme sprigs, halved garlic cloves, sliced onion, chillies, coriander seeds, peppercorns and lemon rind and simmer for 2 minutes.

3 Add the mushrooms to the pan and simmer for 3–4 minutes. Drain the mushrooms through a sieve (strainer), retaining all the herbs and spices, then set aside for a few minutes until thoroughly drained.

4 When the mushrooms have drained, take one large or two small cool sterilized jars and then add a layer of drained mushrooms. Distribute the garlic, onion, herbs and spices evenly among more layers of mushrooms, then add enough olive oil to cover the mixture by at least 1cm/¹/2in. You may need to use extra olive oil if you are making two jars.

5 Leave the pickle to settle, then tap the jars on the work surface to dispel any air bubbles. Seal the jars, then store them in the refrigerator until you are ready to use them. To enjoy this mushroom pickle at its best, you should try to use it within 2 weeks.

Nutritional information per quantity: Energy 579kcal/2392kJ; Protein 9g; Carbohydrate 7.2g, of which sugars 6.2g; Fat 57.4g, of which saturates 8.4g; Cholesterol 0mg; Calcium 33mg; Fibre 5.5g; Sodium 25mg.

Stuffed baby aubergines

This Middle-Eastern fermented pickle makes a succulent and spicy accompaniment to cold meats, but is equally good served with a few salad leaves and bread as a simple appetizer.

MAKES ABOUT 3 JARS

1kg/2¼lb baby aubergines (eggplants)
2 fresh red chillies, halved lengthways
2 fresh green chillies, halved lengthways
2 celery sticks, cut into matchstick strips
2 carrots, cut into matchstick strips
4 garlic cloves, peeled and finely chopped

20ml/4 tsp salt
4 small fresh vine leaves (optional)
750ml/1¼ pints/3 cups cooled
  boiled water
45ml/3 tbsp white wine vinegar

1 Trim the aubergine stems, but do not remove them completely. Cut a slit lengthways along each aubergine, almost through to the other side, in order to make a pocket.

2 Steam the aubergines for 5–6 minutes or until they are just tender when tested with the tip of a sharp knife. Remove the aubergines from the heat, then transfer to a colander set over a bowl. Place a plate on top of the aubergines, then arrange a few weights on the plate to press it down gently. Leave the aubergines weighted down like this for 4 hours in order to squeeze out all the moisture from them.

3 Finely chop two red and two green chilli halves and place in a bowl. Add the celery, carrots, garlic and 5ml/1 tsp of the salt, mix together and use to stuff the aubergine pockets. Tightly pack the aubergines and remaining chillies, and vine leaves if using, into a large sterilized jar.

4 Pour the water into a jug (pitcher) and add the remaining 15ml/1 tbsp salt and the vinegar. Stir together until the salt has dissolved. Pour enough brine into the jar to cover the aubergines, then weigh down the top.

5 Cover the jar with a clean dish towel and leave in a warm, well-ventilated place to ferment. The brine will turn cloudy as fermentation starts, but will clear after 1–2 weeks when the pickle has finished fermenting. As soon as this happens, cover and seal the jar and store in the refrigerator. Eat the pickle within 2 months.

Nutritional information per quantity: Energy 94kcal/401kJ; Protein 4.8g; Carbohydrate 15.5g, of which sugars 14.3g; Fat 2.1g, of which saturates 0.5g; Cholesterol 0mg; Calcium 67mg; Fibre 10.7g; Sodium 35mg.

Dill pickles

Redolent of garlic and piquant with fresh chilli, salty dill pickles can be supple and succulent or crisp and crunchy. Every pickle aficionado has a favourite type.

MAKES ABOUT 900G/2LB

20 small, ridged or knobbly pickling
    (small) cucumbers (or any kind of
    small cucumbers if unavailable)
2 litres/3¹/₂ pints/8 cups water
175g/6oz/³/₄ cup coarse sea salt
15–20 garlic cloves, unpeeled
2 bunches fresh dill
15ml/1 tbsp dill seeds
30ml/2 tbsp mixed pickling spice
1 or 2 hot fresh chillies

1 Scrub the cucumbers and rinse well in cold water. Leave to dry.

2 Put the water and salt in a large heavy pan and bring to the boil. Turn off the heat and leave to cool to room temperature.

3 Lightly crush each garlic clove, breaking the papery skin. Pack the cucumbers tightly into one or two wide-necked, sterilized jars, layering them with the garlic, fresh dill, dill seeds and pickling spice. Add one chilli to each jar.

4 Pour over the cooled brine, making sure that the cucumbers are completely covered. Tap the jars on the work surface to dispel any trapped air bubbles.

5 Cover the jars with lids and then leave to stand at room temperature for 4–7 days before serving. Store in the refrigerator.

Nutritional information per quantity:
Energy 76kcal/305kJ; Protein 5.3g; Carbohydrate 11.4g, of which sugars 10.7g; Fat 0.8g, of which saturates 0g; Cholesterol 0mg; Calcium 140mg; Fibre 4.6g; Sodium 10,013mg.

Preserved lemons

These richly flavoured fruits are widely used in Middle-Eastern cooking. Only the rind, which contains the essential flavour of the lemon, is used in recipes.

MAKES ABOUT 2 JARS

10 unwaxed lemons
about 200ml/7fl oz/scant 1 cup fresh lemon juice or a combination of fresh and preserved juice
sea salt
boiling water

1 Wash the unwaxed lemons well under cold, running water and then cut each lemon into six to eight wedges.

2 Press a generous amount of sea salt on to the cut surface of each lemon wedge.

3 Pack the salted lemon wedges tightly into two 1.2-litre/2-pint/5-cup warmed sterilized jars, then add 30–45ml/ 2–3 tbsp sea salt to each jar. Pour in half of the lemon juice, then top up with enough boiling water to cover the lemon wedges.

4 Seal the jars and leave them to stand for 2–4 weeks before using.

5 To use, drain off the juice that has been used to preserve the lemons and reserve it (this salty, well-flavoured juice can be used to flavour salad dressings or added to a variety of hot sauces, so it is well worth saving).

6 Rinse the preserved lemons well to remove some of the salty flavour, then pull off and discard the flesh. Cut the lemon rind into strips or leave in chunks and use as desired.

Nutritional information per quantity:
 Energy 48kcal/198kJ; Protein 2.5g; Carbohydrate 8g, of which sugars 8g; Fat 0.8g, of which saturates 0.3g; Cholesterol 0mg; Calcium 213mg; Fibre 0g; Sodium 13mg.

Sweet pickled watermelon rind

This unusual pickle has an aromatic melon flavour and a crunchy texture. It's a perfect way to use up the part of the fruit that is normally discarded.

MAKES ABOUT 900G/2LB

900g/2lb watermelon rind
  (from 1 large fruit)
50g/2oz/1/4 cup salt
900ml/1 1/2 pints/3 3/4 cups water
450g/1lb/2 1/4 cups preserving or
  granulated (white) sugar

300ml/1/2 pint/1 1/4 cups white wine
  vinegar
6 whole cloves
7.5cm/3in cinnamon stick

1 Remove the dark green skin from the watermelon rind, leaving a thin layer, no more than 3mm/1/8in thick, of the pink fruit. Cut the rind into slices about 5cm x 5mm/2 x 1/4in thick, and place in a large bowl.

2 Dissolve the salt in 600ml/1 pint/2 1/2 cups of the water. Add the watermelon rind, cover and leave for at least 6 hours or overnight.

3 Drain the watermelon rind and rinse under cold water. Put the rind in a pan and cover with fresh water. Bring to the boil, reduce the heat and simmer for 10–15 minutes until just tender. Drain well.

4 Put the sugar, vinegar and remaining water in a clean pan. Tie the cloves and cinnamon in muslin (cheesecloth) and add to the pan. Heat gently, stirring occasionally, until the sugar has dissolved, then bring to the boil and simmer for 10 minutes. Turn off the heat. Add the rind, cover and leave to stand for about 2 hours.

5 Slowly bring the mixture back to the boil, then reduce the heat and simmer gently for 20 minutes, or until the rind has a translucent appearance. Remove the pan from the heat and discard the spice bag.

6 Transfer the watermelon rind to hot sterilized jars. Pour over the hot syrup, tapping the jar to release any trapped air. Cover and seal. Leave to mature for at least 4 weeks before eating. This really helps the flavours to develop.

Nutritional information per quantity: Energy 1836kcal/7834kJ; Protein 6.8g; Carbohydrate 478.3g, of which sugars 478.3g; Fat 1.8g, of which saturates 0g; Cholesterol 0mg; Calcium 608mg; Fibre 9.9g; Sodium 567mg.

Pickled limes

This hot, pungent pickle comes from the Punjab in India. Salting softens the rind and intensifies the flavour of the limes, while they mature in the first month or two of storage.

MAKES ABOUT 1KG/2¼LB

1kg/2¼lb unwaxed limes
75g/3oz/⅓ cup salt
seeds from 6 green cardamom pods
5ml/1 tsp cumin seeds
6 whole cloves
4 fresh red chillies, seeded and sliced
5cm/2in piece fresh root ginger, peeled
    and finely shredded
450g/1lb/2¼ cups preserving or
    granulated (white) sugar

1 Put the limes in a large bowl and pour over cold water to cover. Leave to soak for 8 hours, or overnight if preferred.

2 The next day, remove the limes from the water. Using a sharp knife, cut each lime in half from end to end, then cut each half into 5mm/¼in-thick slices. Place the lime slices in the bowl, sprinkling the salt between the layers. Cover and leave to stand for a further 8 hours.

3 Drain the limes, catching the juices in a preserving pan. Crush the cardamom seeds with the cumin seeds. Add to the pan with the cloves, chillies, ginger and sugar. Bring to the boil, stirring until the sugar dissolves. Reduce the heat, then simmer for 2 minutes. Remove from the heat and leave to cool.

4 Mix the limes in the syrup. Pack into sterilized jars, cover and seal. Store in a cool, dark place for at least 1 month before eating. Use within 1 year.

Nutritional information per quantity: Energy 1963kcal/8354kJ; Protein 12.3g; Carbohydrate 502.3g, of which sugars 502.3g; Fat 3g, of which saturates 1g; Cholesterol 0mg; Calcium 1089mg; Fibre 0g; Sodium 2042mg.

Pickled plums

This preserve is popular in Central Europe and works well for all varieties of plums, from small wild bullaces and astringent damsons to the more delicately flavoured mirabelles.

MAKES ABOUT 900G/2LB

900g/2lb firm plums
150ml/¼ pint/²/₃ cup clear apple juice
450ml/¾ pint/scant 2 cups cider vinegar
2.5ml/½ tsp salt
8 allspice berries (or juniper berries if unavailable)
2.5cm/1in piece fresh root ginger, peeled and cut into matchstick strips
4 bay leaves
675g/1½lb/scant 3½ cups preserving or granulated (white) sugar

1 Wash the plums, then prick them once or twice using a wooden cocktail stick (toothpick). Put the apple juice, cider vinegar, salt, allspice berries, strips of ginger and the bay leaves in a preserving pan.

2 Add the plums to the pan and slowly bring to the boil. Reduce the heat and simmer gently for 10 minutes, or until the plums are just tender. Remove the plums with a slotted spoon and pack them into hot sterilized jars.

3 Add the preserving or granulated sugar to the pan and then stir over a low heat until dissolved. Continue to cook, boiling steadily, for about 10 minutes, or until the mixture has become syrupy.

4 Remove the pan from the heat, leave the syrup to cool for a few minutes, then pour it over the plums in the jars. Cover the jars and seal them. Store for at least 1 month before using and then use them within 1 year.

Nutritional information per quantity: Energy 3041kcal/12,988kJ; Protein 8.9g; Carbohydrate 799.4g, of which sugars 799.4g; Fat 1.1g, of which saturates 0g; Cholesterol 0mg; Calcium 485mg; Fibre 14.4g; Sodium 61mg.

Striped spiced oranges

These delightful sweet-sour spiced orange slices have a wonderfully warming flavour and look very pretty. Serve them with baked ham, rich terrines and gamey pâtés. They are also delicious with roasted red peppers and grilled halloumi cheese.

MAKES ABOUT 1.2KG/2½LB

6 small or medium oranges
750ml/1¼ pints/3 cups white wine vinegar
900g/2lb/4½ cups preserving or
   granulated (white) sugar

7.5cm/3in cinnamon stick
5ml/1 tsp whole allspice
8 whole cloves
45ml/3 tbsp brandy (optional)

1 Scrub the oranges well, then cut strips of rind from each one using a canelle knife (zester) to achieve a striped effect. Reserve the strips of rind.

2 Using a sharp knife, cut the oranges across into slices slightly thicker than 5mm/¼in. Remove and discard any pips (seeds).

3 Put the orange slices into a preserving pan and pour over just enough cold water to cover the fruit. Bring to the boil, then reduce the heat and simmer gently for about 5 minutes, or until the oranges are tender. Using a slotted spoon, transfer the orange slices to a large bowl and discard the cooking liquid.

4 Put the vinegar and sugar in the cleaned pan. Tie the cinnamon, whole allspice and orange rind together in muslin (cheesecloth) and add to the pan. Slowly bring to the boil, stirring, until the sugar has dissolved. Simmer for 1 minute.

5 Return the oranges slices to the pan and cook gently for about 30 minutes, or until the rind is translucent and the orange slices look glazed. Remove from the heat and discard the spice bag.

6 Using a slotted spoon, transfer the orange slices to hot sterilized jars, adding the cloves between the layers. Bring the syrup to a rapid boil and boil for about 10 minutes, or until slightly thickened.

7 Allow the syrup to cool for a few minutes, then stir in the brandy if using. Pour the syrup into the jars, making sure that the fruit is completely immersed in the liquid. Gently tap the jars on the work surface to release any air bubbles, then cover and seal them. Store the orange slices for at least 2 weeks before using, and use them within 6 months.

Nutritional information per quantity: Energy 3768kcal/16,077kJ; Protein 11.1g; Carbohydrate 991.5g, of which sugars 991.5g; Fat 0.6g, of which saturates 0g; Cholesterol 0mg; Calcium 759mg; Fibre 10.2g; Sodium 84mg.

Italian mustard fruit pickles

This traditional and popular Italian preserve is made from late summer and autumn fruits, and then left to mature in time for Christmas when it is served with Italian steamed sausage.

MAKES ABOUT 1.2KG/2½LB

450ml/¾ pint/scant 2 cups white
  wine vinegar (or cider vinegar for a
  slightly less tangy pickle)
30ml/2 tbsp mustard seeds
1kg/2¼lb mixed fruit, such as peaches,
  nectarines, apricots, plums, melon,
  figs and cherries
675g/1½lb/scant 3½ cups preserving
  or granulated (white) sugar

1 Put the vinegar and mustard seeds in a pan, bring to the boil, then simmer for 5 minutes. Remove from the heat, cover and leave to infuse for 1 hour. Strain the vinegar into a clean pan and discard the mustard seeds.

2 Prepare the fruit. Wash and pat dry the peaches, nectarines, apricots and plums, then stone (pit) and thickly slice or halve. Cut the melon in half, discard the seeds (pips), then slice into 1cm/½in pieces or scoop into balls using a melon baller. Cut the figs into quarters and remove the stalks from the cherries.

3 Add the sugar to the mustard vinegar and heat gently, stirring occasionally, until the sugar has dissolved completely. Bring to the boil, reduce the heat and simmer for 5 minutes, or until syrupy.

4 Add the fruit to the syrup and poach it over a gentle heat for 5–10 minutes. Some fruit will be ready sooner than others, so lift out as soon as each variety is tender, using a slotted spoon. Pack the fruit into hot sterilized jars.

5 Ladle the hot mustard syrup over the fruit. Cover and seal. Allow the pickles to mature for at least 1 month before eating. Use within 6 months.

Nutritional information per quantity: Energy 3140kcal/13,399kJ; Protein 20.2g; Carbohydrate 813.4g, of which sugars 813.4g; Fat 1.2g, of which saturates 0g; Cholesterol 0mg; Calcium 442mg; Fibre 14.4g; Sodium 53mg.

Blushing pears

As this pickle matures, the fruits absorb the colour of the vinegar, giving them a glorious pink hue. They're especially good served with cold turkey, game pie, well-flavoured cheese or pâté.

MAKES ABOUT 1.3KG/3LB

1 small lemon
450g/1lb/2¼ cups golden
  granulated sugar
475ml/16fl oz/2 cups raspberry vinegar
7.5cm/3in cinnamon stick
6 whole cloves
6 allspice berries
150ml/¼ pint/²/₃ cup water
900g/2lb firm pears

1 Using a sharp knife, thinly pare a few strips of rind from the lemon. Squeeze out 30ml/2 tbsp of the juice and put it in a pan with the strips of rind.

2 Add the sugar, vinegar, spices and water to the pan. Heat gently, stirring occasionally, until the sugar has dissolved, then slowly bring to the boil.

3 Meanwhile, prepare the pears. Peel and halve the pears, then scoop out the cores using a melon baller or small teaspoon. Discard the cores. If the pears are very large, cut them into quarters rather than halves.

4 Add the pears to the pan and simmer very gently for about 20 minutes, or until tender and translucent but still whole. Check the pears frequently towards the end of the cooking time. Using a slotted spoon, remove the pears from the pan and pack into hot sterilized jars, adding the spices and strips of lemon rind.

5 Boil the syrup for 5 minutes, or until slightly reduced. Skim off any scum, then ladle the syrup over the pears. Cover and seal. Store for at least 1 month before eating.

Nutritional information per quantity: Energy 2133kcal/9086kJ; Protein 5g; Carbohydrate 560.3g, of which sugars 560.3g; Fat 0.9g, of which saturates 0g; Cholesterol 0mg; Calcium 338mg; Fibre 19.8g; Sodium 54mg.

Sweet and hot dried fruit chutney

This rich, thick and slightly sticky preserve of spiced dried fruit is a wonderful way to enliven cold roast turkey left over from Christmas or Thanksgiving dinners.

MAKES ABOUT 1.5KG/3LB 6OZ

350g/12oz/1¹/₂ cups ready-to-eat
  dried apricots
225g/8oz/1¹/₃ cups dried dates,
  stoned (pitted)
225g/8oz/1¹/₃ cups dried figs
50g/2oz/¹/₃ cup glacé (candied)
  citrus peel
150g/5oz/1 cup raisins
50g/2oz/¹/₂ cup dried cranberries
  (or dried sour cherries)

120ml/4fl oz/¹/₂ cup cranberry juice
  (or apple juice)
400ml/14fl oz/1²/₃ cups cider vinegar
225g/8oz/1 cup demerara (raw) sugar
finely grated rind and juice of 1 lemon
5ml/1 tsp mixed spice (apple pie spice)
5ml/1 tsp ground coriander
5ml/1 tsp cayenne pepper
5ml/1 tsp salt

1 Roughly chop the dried apricots, dates, figs and citrus peel, then put all the dried fruit in a preserving pan. Pour over the cranberry juice, stir, then cover and leave to soak for 2 hours, or until the fruit has absorbed most of the juice.

2 Add the cider vinegar and demerara sugar to the pan, then stir the mixture over a low heat until the sugar has dissolved.

3 Bring the mixture to the boil, then reduce the heat and simmer for about 30 minutes, or until the fruit is soft and the chutney fairly thick. Stir occasionally during cooking.

4 Stir in the lemon rind and juice, and the mixed spice, coriander, cayenne pepper and salt. Simmer for a further 15 minutes, stirring frequently towards the end of the cooking, until the chutney is thick and no excess liquid remains.

5 Spoon the chutney into warmed sterilized jars, then cover them and seal tightly. Store the jars in a cool, dark place and leave the chutney to mature for at least 1 month before eating, in order to allow the flavours to develop. Use the chutney within 1 year. Once opened, store the jars in the refrigerator and use within 2 months.

Nutritional information per quantity: Energy 2998kcal/12,789kJ; Protein 31.9g; Carbohydrate 746.7g, of which sugars 729.4g; Fat 7.1g, of which saturates 0g; Cholesterol 0mg; Calcium 1157mg; Fibre 51.4g; Sodium 458mg.

Green grape chutney

A hint of lime heightens the fragrant grape flavour and complements the sweetness of this chutney. It is delicious warmed with a knob of butter and served with roast pork.

MAKES 1.2KG/2½LB

900g/2lb/6 cups seedless green grapes
900g/2lb tart cooking apples
450g/1lb/2¼ cups sugar
450ml/¾ pint/scant 2 cups white
  wine vinegar
finely grated rind and juice of 1 lime
1.5ml/¼ tsp salt

1 Halve the grapes if large, then peel, core and finely chop the apples. Put the fruit in a preserving pan with the sugar and vinegar and slowly bring to the boil.

2 Reduce the heat and simmer the chutney for about 45 minutes, or until the fruit is tender and the chutney fairly thick.

3 Stir the lime rind and juice, and the salt, into the chutney. Simmer for 15 minutes until the chutney is thick and no excess liquid remains.

4 Spoon the chutney into warmed sterilized jars, cover and seal. Store in a cool, dark place and leave to mature for at least 1 month before eating. Use within 18 months.

Nutritional information per quantity: Energy 2628kcal/11,237kJ; Protein 8.6g; Carbohydrate 689g, of which sugars 689g; Fat 1.8g, of which saturates 0g; Cholesterol 0mg; Calcium 392mg; Fibre 20.7g; Sodium 63mg.

Tomato chutney

This spicy and dark, sweet-sour chutney is perfect served with a selection of well-flavoured cheeses, and biscuits or bread, or with cold roast meats such as ham, turkey, tongue or lamb.

MAKES ABOUT 1.8KG/4LB

900g/2lb tomatoes, skinned
225g/8oz/1¹/₂ cups raisins
225g/8oz onions, chopped
225g/8oz/generous 1 cup caster
    (superfine) sugar
600ml/1 pint/2¹/₂ cups malt vinegar

1 Chop the skinned tomatoes roughly and then place them in a preserving pan. Add the raisins, onions and caster sugar.

2 Pour the malt vinegar into the pan and then bring the mixture to the boil. Reduce the heat and simmer for 2 hours, uncovered, until soft and thickened.

3 Remove the chutney from the heat and then transfer to warmed sterilized jars.

4 Top the jars with waxed discs and lids. Store in a cool, dark place and leave to mature for 1 month. The chutney will keep unopened for up to 1 year. Once opened, store the jars in the refrigerator.

Nutritional information per quantity: Energy 1733kcal/7384kJ; Protein 14.9g; Carbohydrate 436.7g, of which sugars 431.6g; Fat 4g, of which saturates 0.9g; Cholesterol 0mg; Calcium 342mg; Fibre 16.6g; Sodium 236mg.

Mango chutney

No Indian meal would be complete without this classic chutney. It's delicious scooped up on crispy fried poppadums. Mango chutney is also great served with chargrilled chicken, turkey or duck breasts, with potato wedges and soured cream, or spread on cheese on toast.

MAKES ABOUT 1KG/2¼LB

900g/2lb mangoes, halved, peeled
  and stoned (pitted)
2.5ml/½ tsp salt
225g/8oz cooking apples, peeled
300ml/½ pint/1¼ cups distilled
  malt vinegar

200g/7oz/scant 1 cup demerara
  (raw) sugar
1 onion, chopped
1 garlic clove, crushed
10ml/2 tsp ground ginger

1 Using a sharp knife, slice the mango flesh into chunks and place in a large, non-metallic bowl. Sprinkle with salt and set aside while you prepare the apples.

2 Cut the apples into quarters, then remove and discard the cores and peel. Chop the flesh roughly.

3 Put the malt vinegar and sugar in a preserving pan and heat very gently, stirring occasionally, until the sugar has dissolved completely.

4 Add the mangoes, apples, onion, garlic and ginger to the pan and slowly bring the mixture to the boil, stirring occasionally.

5 Reduce the heat and simmer gently for about 1 hour, stirring frequently towards the end of the cooking time, until the chutney is reduced to a thick consistency and no excess liquid remains.

6 Spoon the chutney into warmed sterilized jars, then cover and seal them tightly. Store the jars in a cool, dark place and leave the chutney to mature for at least 2 weeks before eating. Use within 1 year of making.

Nutritional information per quantity: Energy 1401kcal/5997kJ; Protein 8.7g; Carbohydrate 360.7g, of which sugars 356.6g; Fat 2.2g, of which saturates 0.9g; Cholesterol 0mg; Calcium 238mg; Fibre 27.8g; Sodium 1019mg.

Mediterranean chutney

Reminiscent of the warm Mediterranean climate, this mixed vegetable chutney is colourful, mild and warm in flavour and goes particularly well with grilled meats and sausages.

MAKES ABOUT 1.8KG/4LB

450g/1lb Spanish (Bermuda) onions, chopped

900g/2lb ripe tomatoes, skinned and chopped

1 aubergine (eggplant), weighing about 350g/12oz, trimmed and cut into 1cm/¹/₂in cubes

450g/1lb courgettes (zucchini), sliced

1 yellow (bell) pepper, quartered, seeded and sliced

1 red (bell) pepper, quartered, seeded and sliced

3 garlic cloves, crushed

1 small sprig of rosemary

1 small sprig of thyme

2 bay leaves

15ml/1 tbsp salt

15ml/1 tbsp paprika

300ml/¹/₂ pint/1¹/₄ cups malt vinegar

400g/14oz/2 cups sugar

1 Put the onions, tomatoes, aubergine, courgettes, peppers and garlic in a pan. Cover and heat gently, stirring, for 15 minutes, or until the juices start to run. Tie the rosemary, thyme and bay leaves in a piece of muslin (cheesecloth), then add to the pan with the salt, paprika and half the vinegar.

2 Simmer, uncovered, for about 25 minutes until the vegetables are tender and the juices reduced. Add the remaining vinegar and the sugar, and stir over a low heat until the sugar has dissolved.

3 Simmer gently for 30 minutes, stirring frequently towards the end of the cooking time. When the chutney is reduced to a thick consistency and no liquid remains, discard the herbs, then spoon into warmed sterilized jars.

4 Set the jars of chutney aside until cool, then cover and seal with vinegar-proof lids. Store the jars in a cool, dark place and allow to mature for at least 2 months before eating. Use within 2 years. Once opened, store in the refrigerator and use within 2 months.

Nutritional information per quantity: Energy 2114kcal/8986kJ; Protein 27.1g; Carbohydrate 516.4g, of which sugars 504.1g; Fat 7.6g, of which saturates 1.9g; Cholesterol 0mg; Calcium 549mg; Fibre 28.9g; Sodium 6036mg.

Butternut, apricot and almond chutney

Coriander seeds and turmeric add a slightly spicy touch to this rich golden chutney. It is delicious in little canapés or with cubes of mozzarella cheese; it is also good in sandwiches.

MAKES ABOUT 1.8KG/4LB

1 small butternut squash, weighing about 800g/1³⁄₄lb (or a wedge of pumpkin weighing 500g/1¹⁄₄lb)
400g/14oz/2 cups golden granulated sugar
600ml/1 pint/2¹⁄₂ cups cider vinegar
2 onions, chopped
225g/8oz/1 cup ready-to-eat dried apricots, quartered
finely grated rind and juice of 1 orange
2.5ml/¹⁄₂ tsp turmeric
15ml/1 tbsp coriander seeds
15ml/1 tbsp salt
115g/4oz/1 cup flaked (sliced) almonds

1 Halve the butternut squash lengthways and scoop out the seeds. Peel off the skin, then cut the flesh into 2cm/³⁄₄in cubes.

2 Put the sugar and vinegar in a preserving pan and heat gently, stirring occasionally, until the sugar has dissolved.

3 Add the squash, onions, apricots, orange rind and juice, turmeric, coriander seeds and salt to the preserving pan. Bring the mixture slowly to the boil.

4 Reduce the heat and simmer gently for 45–50 minutes, stirring frequently towards the end of the cooking time, until the chutney is reduced to a thick consistency and no excess liquid remains. Stir in the flaked almonds.

5 Spoon the chutney into warmed sterilized jars, cover and seal. Store in a cool, dark place and allow to mature for at least 1 month before eating. Use within 1 year. Once opened, store in the refrigerator and use within 2 months.

Nutritional information per quantity: Energy 2883kcal/12,195kJ; Protein 45.7g; Carbohydrate 557.3g, of which sugars 541g; Fat 67.9g, of which saturates 5.9g; Cholesterol 0mg; Calcium 986mg; Fibre 36.3g; Sodium 5979mg.

Hot yellow plum chutney

*It is worth seeking out yellow plums to make this hot, fragrant chutney.
Their slightly tart flavour is perfect with deep-fried Asian-style snacks
such as spring rolls and wontons, or battered vegetables and shellfish.*

MAKES 1.3KG/3LB

900g/2lb yellow plums, halved and
  stoned (pitted)
1 onion, finely chopped
7.5cm/3in piece fresh root ginger,
  peeled and grated
3 whole star anise

350ml/12fl oz/1¹/₂ cups white wine
  vinegar
225g/8oz/1 cup soft light brown sugar
5 celery sticks, thinly sliced
3 green chillies, seeded and finely sliced
2 garlic cloves, crushed

1 Put the halved plums, chopped onion, grated ginger and the star anise in
a large pan and pour over half the white wine vinegar. Bring the mixture to
the boil and then simmer gently over a low heat for about 30 minutes, or
until the plums have softened.

2 Stir the remaining white wine vinegar, the brown sugar, sliced celery and
chillies and the crushed garlic into the plum mixture. Cook very gently over
a low heat, stirring frequently, until the sugar has completely dissolved.

3 Bring to the boil, then reduce the heat and simmer for 45–50 minutes, or
until the mixture is thick, with no excess liquid left at the end of the cooking
time. Stir the mixture frequently during the final stages of cooking to prevent
the chutney sticking to the pan.

4 Remove the pan from the heat and then spoon the plum chutney into
warmed sterilized jars with non-metallic lids. Cover the jars and then seal
them immediately.

5 Store the chutney in a cool, dark place and then leave it to mature for at
least 1 month before using in order to allow the flavours to develop. Use the
chutney within 2 years. Once opened, store the chutney in the refrigerator
and use it within 3 months.

Nutritional information per quantity: Energy 1243kcal/5312kJ; Protein 8g; Carbohydrate 320.4g, of which sugars 319g;
Fat 1.3g, of which saturates 0g; Cholesterol 0mg; Calcium 313mg; Fibre 16.9g; Sodium 123mg.

Rhubarb and tangerine chutney

This soft-textured chutney has an attractive colour and a sweet, spicy flavour. It works especially well when partnered with Chinese-style roast duck, or with cold meats such as ham or gammon.

MAKES ABOUT 1.3KG/3LB

1 large onion, finely chopped
300ml/½ pint/1¼ cups distilled
   malt vinegar
4 whole cloves
7.5cm/3in cinnamon stick
1 tangerine, or ½ orange
400g/14oz/2 cups sugar
150g/5oz/1 cup sultanas (golden raisins)
1kg/2¼lb rhubarb, cut into
   2.5cm/1in lengths

1 Put the onion in a preserving pan with the vinegar, whole cloves and cinnamon stick. Bring to the boil, then reduce the heat and simmer for 10 minutes, or until the onions are just tender.

2 Meanwhile, thinly pare the rind from the tangerine or orange (it is often easier to peel the fruit first, then slice the white pith from the rind). Finely shred the rind and add to the pan with the sugar and sultanas. Stir until the sugar has dissolved, then simmer for 10 minutes, or until the syrup is thick.

3 Add the rhubarb to the pan. Cook gently for about 15 minutes, stirring carefully from time to time, until the rhubarb is soft but still retains its shape, and just a little spare liquid remains.

4 Remove the pan from the heat and cool for 10 minutes, then stir gently to distribute the fruit. Spoon the chutney into warmed sterilized jars, cover and seal. Store in a cool, dark place and allow to mature for at least 1 month. Use within 1 year. Once opened, store in the refrigerator use within 2 months.

Nutritional information per quantity: Energy 2215kcal/9455kJ; Protein 20.2g; Carbohydrate 564.6g, of which sugars 555.4g; Fat 2.5g, of which saturates 0g; Cholesterol 0mg; Calcium 1354mg; Fibre 23.1g; Sodium 95mg.

Beetroot and orange preserve

With its vibrant red colour and rich earthy flavour, this distinctive chutney is good with salads as well as full-flavoured cheeses such as mature Cheddar, Stilton or Gorgonzola.

MAKES ABOUT 1.3KG/3LB

350g/12oz raw beetroot (beets)
350g/12oz eating apples
300ml/1/2 pint/11/4 cups malt vinegar
200g/7oz/1 cup sugar
225g/8oz red onions, finely chopped
1 garlic clove, crushed
finely grated rind and juice of 2 oranges
5ml/1 tsp ground allspice
5ml/1 tsp salt

1 Scrub or, if necessary, thinly peel the beetroot, then cut into 1cm/1/2in pieces. Peel, quarter and core the apples and cut into 1cm/1/2in pieces. Alternatively, for speedier preparation and a finer-textured chutney, put the peeled beetroot through the coarse grating blade of a food processor.

2 Put the vinegar and sugar in a preserving pan and heat gently, stirring occasionally, until the sugar has dissolved. Add the beetroot, apples, onions, garlic, orange rind and juice, ground allspice and salt to the pan. Bring to the boil, reduce the heat, then simmer for 40 minutes.

3 Increase the heat slightly and boil for 10 minutes, or until the chutney is thick and no excess liquid remains. Stir frequently to prevent the chutney catching on the base of the pan.

4 Spoon the chutney into warmed sterilized jars, cover and seal. Store in a cool, dark place and allow to mature for at least 2 weeks before eating. Use within 6 months of making. Refrigerate once opened and use within 1 month.

Nutritional information per quantity: Energy 1055kcal/4506kJ; Protein 8.2g; Carbohydrate 271.1g, of which sugars 269g; Fat 0.8g, of which saturates 0g; Cholesterol 0mg; Calcium 195mg; Fibre 12.3g; Sodium 255mg.

Confit of slow-cooked onions

This jam of caramelized onions in balsamic vinegar will keep for several days in a sealed jar in the refrigerator. You can use red, white or yellow onions, but yellow will produce the sweetest result.

MAKES ABOUT 500G/1¼LB

30ml/2 tbsp olive oil
15g/¹/₂oz/1 tbsp butter
500g/1¹/₄lb onions, sliced
salt and ground black pepper
3–5 fresh thyme sprigs
1 fresh bay leaf
30ml/2 tbsp light muscovado (brown)
   sugar, plus a little extra to taste
50g/2oz/¹/₄ cup ready-to-eat
   prunes, chopped
30ml/2 tbsp balsamic vinegar,
   plus a little extra to taste
120ml/4fl oz/¹/₂ cup red wine
60ml/4 tbsp water

1 Reserve 5ml/1 tsp of the oil, then heat the remaining oil with the butter in a large pan. Add the onions, cover and cook gently over a low heat for about 15 minutes, stirring occasionally.

2 Season with salt and ground black pepper, then add the thyme, bay leaf and sugar. Cook slowly, uncovered, for a further 15–20 minutes until the onions are very soft. Stir occasionally to prevent sticking or burning. Add the prunes, vinegar, wine and water to the pan and cook over a low heat, stirring frequently, for 20 minutes, or until most of the liquid has evaporated. Add a little more water and reduce the heat if it looks dry. Remove from the heat.

3 Season, adding more muscovado sugar and/or balsamic vinegar to taste. Leave the confit to cool, then stir in the remaining 5ml/1 tsp olive oil and serve.

Nutritional information per quantity: Energy 678kcal/2827kJ; Protein 7.5g; Carbohydrate 87.9g, of which sugars 76.4g; Fat 35.5g, of which saturates 11g; Cholesterol 32mg; Calcium 161mg; Fibre 9.8g; Sodium 113mg.

Kashmir chutney

In the true tradition of the Kashmiri country store, this is a typical family recipe passed down from generation to generation. It is wonderful served with plain or spicy grilled sausages.

MAKES ABOUT 2.75KG/6LB

1kg/2¹⁄₄lb green eating apples
15g/¹⁄₂oz garlic cloves
1 litre/1³⁄₄ pints/4 cups malt vinegar
450g/1lb dates
115g/4oz preserved stem ginger
450g/1lb/3 cups raisins
450g/1lb/2 cups soft light brown sugar
2.5ml/¹⁄₂ tsp cayenne pepper
30ml/2 tbsp salt

1 Quarter the apples, remove and discard the cores, and then chop the apples coarsely. Peel and chop the garlic.

2 Place the apples and garlic in a pan with enough malt vinegar to cover. Bring the mixture to the boil and then continue to boil for 10 minutes.

3 Chop the dates and the preserved stem ginger and then add them to the pan, together with the raisins, brown sugar, cayenne pepper and salt. Cook the mixture gently for 45 minutes.

4 Remove the pan from the heat, then spoon the mixture into warmed sterilized jars and seal immediately.

Nutritional information per quantity: Energy 3920kcal/16,737kJ; Protein 22.6g; Carbohydrate 1014.4g, of which sugars 1012.2g; Fat 3.3g, of which saturates 0g; Cholesterol 0mg; Calcium 599mg; Fibre 33.7g; Sodium 12139mg.

Chunky pear and walnut chutney

This chutney recipe is ideal for using up hard windfall pears. Its mellow flavour is excellent with cheese and also good with grains such as in pilaff or with tabbouleh.

MAKES ABOUT 1.8KG/4LB

1.2kg/2¹/₂lb firm pears
225g/8oz tart cooking apples
225g/8oz onions
450ml/³/₄ pint/scant 2 cups cider vinegar
175g/6oz/generous 1 cup sultanas
   (golden raisins)

finely grated rind and juice of
  1 orange
400g/14oz/2 cups sugar
115g/4oz/1 cup walnuts, roughly
  chopped
2.5ml/¹/₂ tsp ground cinnamon

1 Peel and core the pears and apples, then chop them into 2.5cm/1in chunks. Peel and quarter the onions, then chop into pieces the same size.

2 Place in a preserving pan with the vinegar. Slowly bring to the boil, then reduce the heat and simmer for 40 minutes, until the apples, pears and onions are tender, stirring the mixture occasionally.

3 Meanwhile, put the sultanas in a bowl, pour over the orange juice and leave to soak. Add the sugar, sultanas, and orange rind and juice to the pan.

4 Gently heat the mixture until the sugar has dissolved, then simmer for 30–40 minutes, or until the chutney is thick and no excess liquid remains. Stir frequntly towards the end of cooking to prevent the chutney sticking on the bottom of the pan.

5 Gently toast the walnuts in a non-stick pan over a low heat, stirring constantly, for 5 minutes, until golden. Stir the nuts into the chutney with the cinnamon.

6 Spoon the chutney into warmed sterilized jars, cover and seal. Store in a cool, dark place, then leave to mature for at least 1 month. Use within 1 year.

Nutritional information per quantity: Energy 3501kcal/14,797kJ; Protein 29.8g; Carbohydrate 705.3g, of which sugars 699.3g; Fat 81.4g, of which saturates 6.4g; Cholesterol 0mg; Calcium 603mg; Fibre 40.7g; Sodium 189mg.

Fiery Bengal chutney

Not for timid tastebuds, this fiery chutney is the perfect choice for lovers of hot and spicy food. Although it can be eaten a month after making, it is better matured for longer.

MAKES ABOUT 2KG/4½LB

115g/4oz fresh root ginger
1kg/2¼lb cooking apples
675g/1½lb onions
6 garlic cloves, finely chopped
225g/8oz/1½ cups raisins
450ml/½ pint/scant 2 cups malt vinegar
400g/14oz/1¾ cups demerara
    (raw) sugar
2 fresh red chillies
2 fresh green chillies
15ml/1 tbsp salt
5ml/1 tsp turmeric

1 Peel and finely shred the fresh root ginger. Peel, core and roughly chop the apples. Peel and quarter the onions, then slice thinly. Place in a preserving pan with the garlic, raisins and vinegar.

2 Bring to the boil, then simmer for 15 minutes, stirring occasionally, until the apples and onions are softened. Add the sugar and stir over a low heat until it has dissolved. Simmer for about 40 minutes, or until thick and pulpy, stirring frequently towards the end of the cooking time.

3 Halve the chillies and remove the seeds, then slice them finely. Add to the pan and cook for a further 10 minutes, or until no excess liquid remains. Stir in the salt and turmeric. Spoon into warmed sterilized jars, cover and seal, then label when cool.

4 Store the chutney in a cool, dark place and leave it to mature for at least 2 months before eating in order to allow the flavours to develop. Use the chutney within 2 years of making. Once opened, store the chutney in the refrigerator and use it within 1 month.

Nutritional information per quantity: Energy 2789kcal/11,889kJ; Protein 18.4g; Carbohydrate 717.3g, of which sugars 701.8g; Fat 3.5g, of which saturates 0g; Cholesterol 0mg; Calcium 573mg; Fibre 31.2g; Sodium 6163mg.

Green tomato chutney

This is a classic chutney for using the last tomatoes of summer that just never seem to ripen. Apples and onions contribute essential flavour, which is enhanced by the addition of spice.

MAKES ABOUT 2.5KG/5½LB

1.8kg/4lb green tomatoes,
   roughly chopped
450g/1lb cooking apples, peeled,
   cored and chopped
450g/1lb onions, chopped
2 large garlic cloves, crushed
15ml/1 tbsp salt
45ml/3 tbsp pickling spice
600ml/1 pint/2½ cups cider vinegar
450g/1lb/2¼ cups sugar

1 Place the tomatoes, apples and onions with the garlic in a pan and add the salt. Tie the pickling spice in a piece of muslin (cheesecloth) and add to the ingredients in the pan.

2 Add half the vinegar and bring to the boil. Reduce the heat and simmer for 1 hour, or until the chutney is reduced and thick, stirring frequently.

3 Put the sugar and remaining vinegar in a pan and heat gently until the sugar has dissolved, then add to the chutney.

4 Simmer over a low heat for about 1½ hours until the chutney is thick, stirring occasionally.

5 Remove the muslin bag, then spoon the hot chutney into warmed sterilized jars. You can also use a long-handled teaspoon to press the mixture down into the jars in order to exclude any trapped air pockets.

6 Cover the chutney with wax discs, and then seal the jars immediately. Allow the chutney to mature for at least 1 month before using.

Nutritional information per quantity: Energy 2398kcal/10,233kJ; Protein 21.6g; Carbohydrate 601.7g, of which sugars 591.3g; Fat 6.8g, of which saturates 1.8g; Cholesterol 0mg; Calcium 495mg; Fibre 31.5g; Sodium 2177mg.

Relishes

These versatile condiments can be fresh

and quick to prepare or rich and slowly

simmered. They usually have bold,

striking flavours with a piquant, sharp

and spicy taste balanced by sweet and

tangy tones. They are perfect for serving

with cheese and cold or grilled meats,

or for jazzing up plain sandwich fillings.

Sweet piccalilli

Undoubtedly one of the most popular relishes, piccalilli can be eaten with grilled sausages, ham or chops, cold meats or a strong, well-flavoured cheese such as Cheddar. It should contain a good selection of fresh crunchy vegetables in a smooth mustard sauce.

MAKES ABOUT 1.8KG/4LB

1 large cauliflower
450g/1lb pickling (pearl) onions
900g/2lb mixed vegetables, such as
    marrow (large zucchini), cucumber,
    French (green) beans
225g/8oz/1 cup salt
2.4 litres/4 pints/10 cups cold water
200g/7oz/1 cup sugar

2 garlic cloves, peeled and crushed
10ml/2 tsp mustard powder
5ml/1 tsp ground ginger
1 litre/1¾ pints/4 cups distilled
    (white) vinegar
25g/1oz/¼ cup plain
    (all-purpose) flour
15ml/1 tbsp turmeric

1 Prepare the vegetables. Divide the cauliflower into small florets; peel and quarter the pickling onions; seed and finely dice the marrow and cucumber; top and tail the French beans, then cut them into 2.5cm/1in lengths.

2 Layer the vegetables in a large glass or stainless-steel bowl, generously sprinkling each layer with salt. Pour over the water, cover the bowl with clear film (plastic wrap) and leave to soak for 24 hours.

3 Drain the soaked vegetables and discard the brine. Rinse well in several changes of cold water to remove as much salt as possible, then drain.

4 Put the sugar, garlic, mustard, ginger and 900ml/1½ pints/3¾ cups of the vinegar in a preserving pan. Heat gently, stirring occasionally, until the sugar has dissolved. Add the vegetables to the pan, bring to the boil, reduce the heat and simmer for 10–15 minutes, or until they are almost tender.

5 Mix the flour and turmeric with the remaining vinegar and stir into the vegetables. Bring to the boil, stirring, and simmer for 5 minutes, until the piccalilli is thick.

6 Spoon the piccalilli into warmed sterilized jars, cover and seal. Store in a cool, dark place for at least 2 weeks. Use within 1 year.

Nutritional information per quantity: Energy 1358kcal/5757kJ; Protein 34.1g; Carbohydrate 300.8g, of which sugars 266g; Fat 12g, of which saturates 1.2g; Cholesterol 0mg; Calcium 555mg; Fibre 20.6g; Sodium 4011mg.

Tart tomato relish

Adding lime to this relish gives it a wonderfully tart, tangy flavour and a pleasantly sour after-taste. It is particularly good served with grilled or roast meats such as pork or lamb.

MAKES ABOUT 500G/1¼LB

2 pieces preserved stem ginger
1 lime
450g/1lb cherry tomatoes
115g/4oz/¹/₂ cup muscovado
  (molasses) sugar
120ml/4fl oz/¹/₂ cup white wine vinegar
5ml/1 tsp salt

1 Coarsely chop the preserved stem ginger. Slice the lime thinly, including the rind, then chop the slices into small pieces.

2 Place the cherry tomatoes, sugar, vinegar, salt, ginger and lime in a large heavy pan.

3 Bring the mixture to the boil, stirring until the sugar dissolves, then simmer rapidly for about 45 minutes. Stir frequently until the liquid has evaporated and the relish is thick and pulpy.

4 Leave the relish to cool for about 5 minutes, then spoon into sterilized jars. Leave to cool, then cover and store in the refrigerator for up to 1 month.

Nutritional information per quantity: Energy 530kcal/2262kJ; Protein 3.7g; Carbohydrate 134.1g, of which sugars 134.1g; Fat 1.4g, of which saturates 0.5g; Cholesterol 0mg; Calcium 93mg; Fibre 4.5g; Sodium 2012mg.

Yellow pepper and coriander relish

Fresh relishes are quick and easy to make although they do not have a long shelf life. Try this relish with mild, creamy cheeses or with grilled tuna or other firm fish, poultry or meat.

MAKES 1 SMALL JAR

1 large yellow (bell) pepper (if
   unavailable, red and orange sweet
   peppers work just as well as yellow,
   but green peppers are unsuitable
   because they are not sweet enough
   in flavour)
45ml/3 tbsp sesame oil
1 large mild fresh red chilli
small handful of fresh coriander
   (cilantro)
salt

1 Seed and coarsely chop the yellow pepper. Heat the oil in a pan, add the pepper and cook, stirring frequently, for 8–10 minutes, until lightly coloured.

2 Meanwhile, seed the chilli, slice it very thinly and set aside. Transfer the pepper to a food processor and process until chopped, but not puréed. Transfer half the pepper to a bowl, leaving the rest in the food processor.

3 Using a sharp knife, chop the fresh coriander, then add it to the food processor and process briefly to combine. Tip the mixture into the bowl with the rest of the chopped pepper, then add the sliced chilli and stir to combine.

4 Season the relish with salt to taste and stir well to combine. Cover the bowl with clear film (plastic wrap) and chill in the refrigerator until ready to serve. This relish does not keep well, so use it within 3 or 4 days.

Nutritional information per quantity: Energy 313kcal/1292kJ; Protein 2.8g; Carbohydrate 10g, of which sugars 9.5g; Fat 29.3g, of which saturates 4.3g; Cholesterol 0mg; Calcium 28mg; Fibre 2.4g; Sodium 10mg.

Cool cucumber and green tomato relish

This is a great way to use up those green tomatoes that seem as though they're never going to ripen. Combined with cucumber, they make a pale green relish that is great for barbecues.

MAKES ABOUT 1.6KG/3¹/₂LB

2 cucumbers
900g/2lb green tomatoes
4 onions
7.5ml/1¹/₂ tsp salt
350ml/12fl oz/1¹/₂ cups distilled
  (white) vinegar
150g/5oz/scant ³/₄ cup demerara (raw)
  sugar
200g/7oz/1 cup granulated (white) sugar
15ml/1 tbsp plain (all-purpose) flour
2.5ml/¹/₂ tsp mustard powder

1 Wash the cucumbers and green tomatoes. Cut into 1cm/¹/₂in cubes. Peel and finely chop the onions. Layer the vegetables in a strainer placed over a bowl, sprinkling each layer with salt. Cover and leave to drain for at least 6 hours.

2 Discard the salty liquid and tip the vegetables into a large, heavy pan. Reserve 30ml/2 tbsp of the vinegar and add the rest to the pan with the demerara and granulated sugars. Bring to the boil, stirring, until the sugar has dissolved completely. Reduce the heat and cook, uncovered, for 30 minutes, until tender.

3 Blend the flour and mustard to a paste with the reserved vinegar. Stir into the relish and simmer for about 20 minutes, or until the mixture is very thick.

4 Remove from the heat, then spoon into warmed sterilized jars, cover and seal. Store in a cool, dark place for at least 1 week. Use within 6 months.

Nutritional information per quantity: Energy 1803kcal/7668kJ; Protein 18.3g; Carbohydrate 450.8g, of which sugars 427.5g; Fat 4.3g, of which saturates 0.9g; Cholesterol 0mg; Calcium 466mg; Fibre 18.9g; Sodium 129mg.

Bloody Mary relish

This fresh-tasting relish with contrasting textures of tomatoes, celery and cucumber is perfect for al fresco summer eating. For a special occasion, serve it with freshly shucked oysters.

MAKES ABOUT 1.3KG/3LB

1.3kg/3lb ripe well-flavoured tomatoes
1 large cucumber
30–45ml/2–3 tbsp salt
2 celery sticks, chopped
2 garlic cloves, peeled and crushed
175ml/6fl oz/³⁄4 cup white wine vinegar
15ml/1 tbsp sugar
60ml/4 tbsp vodka
5ml/1 tsp Tabasco sauce
10ml/2 tsp Worcestershire sauce

1 Skin and chop the tomatoes. Peel the cucumber and slice the flesh from around the seeds. Discard the seeds and chop the flesh. Layer the vegetables in a colander placed over a bowl, sprinkling each layer with salt. Cover, put in the refrigerator and drain overnight.

2 The next day, rinse thoroughly in cold water to remove as much salt as possible. Drain, then place in a pan. Discard the salty liquid.

3 Add the celery, garlic, vinegar and sugar to the pan and bring to the boil over a low heat. Cook, uncovered, for about 30 minutes, stirring occasionally, until the vegetables have softened and most of the liquid has evaporated.

4 Remove from the heat and cool for 5 minutes. Add the vodka, and the Tabasco and Worcestershire sauces and stir to combine. Spoon into warmed sterilized jars, then cool, cover and seal. Store in the refrigerator for at least 1 week.

Nutritional information per quantity: Energy 430kcal/1814kJ; Protein 13.1g; Carbohydrate 65.6g, of which sugars 65g; Fat 4.5g, of which saturates 1.3g; Cholesterol 0mg; Calcium 233mg; Fibre 16.7g; Sodium 289mg.

Carrot and almond relish

This is a Middle-Eastern classic, usually made with long fine strands of carrot, available from many supermarkets. Alternatively, grate large carrots lengthways on a medium grater.

MAKES ABOUT 675G/1½LB

15ml/1 tbsp coriander seeds
500g/1¼lb carrots, grated
50g/2oz fresh root ginger, finely
   shredded
200g/7oz/1 cup caster (superfine) sugar
finely grated rind and juice of 1 lemon
125ml/4fl oz/½ cup white wine vinegar
75ml/5 tbsp water
30ml/2 tbsp clear honey
7.5ml/1½ tsp salt
50g/2oz/½ cup flaked (sliced) almonds

1 Crush the coriander seeds using a mortar and pestle. Put them in a bowl with the carrots, ginger, sugar and lemon rind and mix together well. Put the lemon juice, vinegar, water, honey and salt in a jug (pitcher) and stir until the salt has dissolved. Pour over the carrot mixture. Mix well, cover and leave in the refrigerator for 4 hours.

2 Transfer the mixture to a preserving pan. Slowly bring to the boil, then reduce the heat and simmer for 15 minutes until the carrots are tender. Increase the heat and boil for 15 minutes, or until most of the liquid has evaporated and the mixture is thick. Stir frequently towards the end of the cooking time to prevent the mixture from sticking to the pan.

3 Put the almonds in a frying pan and toast over a low heat until just beginning to colour. Gently stir into the relish, taking care not to break the almonds.

4 Spoon the relish into warmed sterilized jars, cover and seal. Leave for at least 1 month and use within 18 months. Once opened, store in the refrigerator.

Nutritional information per quantity: Energy 1359kcal/5743kJ; Protein 14.9g; Carbohydrate 275.3g, of which sugars 271.5g; Fat 29.5g, of which saturates 2.7g; Cholesterol 0mg; Calcium 374mg; Fibre 16.2g; Sodium 3125mg.

Lemon and garlic relish

This powerful relish is flavoured with North African spices and punchy preserved lemons, which are widely available in Middle Eastern stores. It is great served with Moroccan tagines.

MAKES 1 SMALL JAR

45ml/3 tbsp olive oil

3 large red onions, sliced

2 heads of garlic, separated into cloves
   and peeled

10ml/2 tsp coriander seeds, crushed

10ml/2 tsp light muscovado (brown)
   sugar, plus a little extra to taste

pinch of saffron threads

5cm/2in piece cinnamon stick

2–3 small whole dried red
   chillies (optional)

2 fresh bay leaves

30–45ml/2–3 tbsp sherry vinegar

juice of 1/2 small orange

30ml/2 tbsp chopped preserved lemon

salt and ground black pepper

1 Gently heat the oil in a large heavy pan. Add the onions and stir, then cover and cook on the lowest setting for 10–15 minutes, stirring occasionally, until soft. Add the garlic cloves and the coriander seeds. Cover the pan and cook for 5–8 minutes, until soft. Add a pinch of salt, lots of ground black pepper and the sugar to the onions and cook, uncovered, for a further 5 minutes.

2 Soak the saffron threads in about 45ml/3 tbsp warm water for 5 minutes, then add to the onions, with the soaking water. Add the cinnamon, chillies if using, and bay leaves. Stir in 30ml/2 tbsp of the vinegar and the orange juice. Cook very gently, uncovered, until the onions are very soft and most of the liquid has evaporated. Stir in the preserved lemon. Cook gently for 5 minutes.

3 Taste the relish and adjust the seasoning, adding more salt, sugar and/or vinegar to taste. Remove the pan from the heat, then serve warm or cold (not hot or chilled). The relish tastes best if left to stand for 24 hours. You can store it in a tightly covered jar for up to a week in the refrigerator, but allow it to stand at room temperature for about an hour before serving.

Nutritional information per quantity: Energy 102kcal/422kJ; Protein 1.9g; Carbohydrate 11.4g, of which sugars 7.8g; Fat 5.7g, of which saturates 0.8g; Cholesterol 0mg; Calcium 28mg; Fibre 1.7g; Sodium 4mg.

Cranberry and red onion relish

This wine-enriched relish is perfect for serving with hot roast turkey at Christmas or Thanksgiving. It is also good served with cold meats or stirred into a beef or game casserole for a touch of sweetness. It can be made several months in advance of the festive season.

MAKES ABOUT 900G/2LB

450g/1lb small red onions
30ml/2 tbsp olive oil
225g/8oz/1 cup soft light brown sugar
450g/1lb/4 cups fresh or
     frozen cranberries
120ml/4fl oz/^{1}/2 cup red wine vinegar

120ml/4fl oz/^{1}/2 cup red wine
15ml/1 tbsp mustard seeds
2.5ml/^{1}/2 tsp ground ginger
30ml/2 tbsp orange liqueur or port
salt and ground black pepper

1 Cut the red onions in half and then slice them very thinly. Heat the olive oil in a large pan, add the sliced onions and then cook them over a very low heat for about 15 minutes, stirring occasionally, until they have softened.

2 Add 30ml/2 tbsp of the sugar and cook for a further 5 minutes, or until the onions are caramelized.

3 Meanwhile, put the cranberries in a pan with the remaining sugar, and the vinegar, red wine, mustard seeds and ginger. Heat gently until the sugar has dissolved, then cover the pan and bring to the boil. It is very important to cover the pan when cooking the cranberries because they can sometimes pop out of the pan during cooking and are very hot. Simmer the relish mixture for 12–15 minutes, until the berries have burst and are tender, then stir in the caramelized onions.

4 Increase the heat slightly and cook uncovered for a further 10 minutes, stirring the mixture frequently until it is well reduced and thickened. Remove the pan from the heat, then season with salt and pepper to taste.

5 Transfer the relish to warmed sterilized jars. Spoon a little of the orange liqueur or port over the top of each, then cover and seal. Store the jars in a cool place for up to 6 months. Once opened, you should store the jars in the refrigerator and then use them within 1 month.

Nutritional information per quantity: Energy 1532kcal/6486kJ; Protein 8g; Carbohydrate 314.6g, of which sugars 304.2g; Fat 23.3g, of which saturates 3.2g; Cholesterol 0mg; Calcium 259mg; Fibre 13.5g; Sodium 46mg.

Red hot relish

Make this relish during the summer months when tomatoes and peppers are plentiful. It enhances simple, plain dishes such as a cheese or mushroom omelette.

MAKES ABOUT 1.3KG/3LB

800g/1¾lb ripe tomatoes, skinned
    and quartered
450g/1lb red onions, chopped
3 red (bell) peppers, seeded and chopped
3 fresh red chillies, seeded and
    finely sliced
200g/7oz/1 cup sugar
200ml/7fl oz/scant 1 cup red
    wine vinegar
30ml/2 tbsp mustard seeds
10ml/2 tsp celery seeds
15ml/1 tbsp paprika
5ml/1 tsp salt

1 Put the chopped tomatoes, onions, peppers and chillies in a preserving pan, cover with a lid and cook over a very low heat for about 10 minutes, stirring once or twice, until the tomato juices start to run.

2 Add the sugar and vinegar to the tomato mixture and slowly bring to the boil, stirring occasionally, until the sugar has dissolved completely. Add the mustard seeds, celery seeds, paprika and salt and then stir well to combine.

3 Increase the heat slightly. Cook, uncovered, for 30 minutes, or until most of the liquid has evaporated and the mixture is thick but moist. Stir frequently towards the end of cooking to prevent the mixture sticking to the pan.

4 Spoon into warmed sterilized jars, cover and seal. Store in a cool, dark place and leave to mature for at least 2 weeks before eating. Use within 1 year. Once opened, refrigerate and use within 2 months.

Nutritional information per quantity: Energy 1270kcal/5392kJ; Protein 17.8g; Carbohydrate 306.2g, of which sugars 294.1g; Fat 5.6g, of which saturates 1.4g; Cholesterol 0mg; Calcium 320mg; Fibre 23.5g; Sodium 121mg.

Plum and cherry relish

This sweet-and-sour fruity relish complements rich poultry, game or meat such as roast duck.
Strain a few spoonfuls into a sauce or gravy to add fruity zest and flavour, as well as colour.

MAKES ABOUT 350G/12OZ

350g/12oz dark-skinned red plums
350g/12oz/2 cups cherries
2 shallots, peeled and finely chopped
15ml/1 tbsp olive oil
30ml/2 tbsp dry sherry
60ml/4 tbsp red wine vinegar
15ml/1 tbsp balsamic vinegar
1 bay leaf
90g/3¹/₂oz/scant ¹/₂ cup demerara
    (raw) sugar

1 Halve and stone (pit) the plums, then roughly chop the flesh. Stone all the cherries.

2 Cook the chopped shallots gently in the olive oil for 5 minutes, or until they are soft. Add the chopped plums and cherries. Pour in the sherry, and vinegars, then add the bay leaf and sugar.

3 Bring to the boil, stirring until the sugar has dissolved. Increase the heat and then cook briskly for about 15 minutes, or until the relish is thick and the fruit is tender. Remove from the heat, then discard the bay leaf.

4 Spoon into warmed sterilized jars. Cover and seal tightly. Store in the refrigerator and use within 3 months.

Nutritional information per quantity: Energy 804kcal/3407kJ; Protein 6.5g; Carbohydrate 170.3g, of which sugars 168.9g; Fat 11.8g, of which saturates 1.6g; Cholesterol 0mg; Calcium 156mg; Fibre 9.6g; Sodium 21mg.

Mango and papaya relish

Brightly coloured pieces of dried papaya add taste and texture to this anise-spiced mango preserve. The fruit is cooked for only a short time to retain its juicy texture and fresh flavour.

MAKES ABOUT 800G/1¾LB

115g/4oz/¹/₂ cup dried papaya

30ml/2 tbsp orange juice or apple juice

2 large, slightly underripe mangoes

2 shallots, very finely sliced

4cm/1¹/₂ in piece fresh root ginger, grated

1 garlic clove, crushed

2 whole star anise

150ml/¹/₄ pint/²/₃ cup cider vinegar

75g/3oz/scant ¹/₂ cup light muscovado (brown) sugar

1.5ml/¹/₄ tsp salt

1 Using a sharp knife or scissors, roughly chop the papaya and place in a small bowl. Sprinkle over the orange juice or apple juice and leave to soak for at least 10 minutes.

2 Meanwhile, peel and slice the mangoes, cutting the flesh away from the stone (pit) in large slices. Cut into 1cm/¹/₂in chunks, then set the flesh aside.

3 Put the sliced shallots, ginger, garlic and star anise in a large pan. Pour over the vinegar. Slowly bring to the boil, then reduce the heat, cover and simmer for 5 minutes, or until the shallots are just beginning to soften.

4 Add the sugar and salt to the pan and stir over a low heat until dissolved. When the mixture is simmering, add the papaya and mangoes and cook for a further 20 minutes, or until the fruit is just tender and the relish mixture has reduced and thickened.

5 Allow the relish to cool for about 5 minutes, then spoon into warmed sterilized jars. Allow to cool completely before covering and sealing. Store in a cool, dark place and use within 3 months of making. Once opened, keep the jars in the refrigerator and use within 1 month.

Nutritional information per quantity: Energy 621kcal/2654kJ; Protein 4.6g; Carbohydrate 158.5g, of which sugars 157.6g; Fat 1g, of which saturates 0.3g; Cholesterol 0mg; Calcium 171mg; Fibre 16.6g; Sodium 623mg.

Corn relish

When golden corn cobs are in season, try preserving their kernels in this delicious relish. It has a lovely crunchy texture and a wonderfully bright, appetizing appearance.

MAKES ABOUT 1KG/2¼LB

6 large fresh corn on the cob

½ small white cabbage, weighing about
    275g/10oz, very finely shredded

2 small onions, halved and very
    finely sliced

475ml/16fl oz/2 cups distilled
    malt vinegar

200g/7oz/1 cup golden granulated sugar

1 red (bell) pepper, seeded and
    finely chopped

5ml/1 tsp salt

15ml/1 tbsp plain (all-purpose) flour

5ml/1 tsp mustard powder

2.5ml/½ tsp turmeric

1 Put the corn in a pan of boiling water and cook for 2 minutes. Drain and, when cool enough to handle, use a sharp knife to strip the kernels from the cobs.

2 Put the kernels in a pan with the cabbage and onions. Reserve 30ml/2 tbsp of the vinegar, then add the rest to the pan with the sugar. Bring to the boil, stirring occasionally until the sugar dissolves. Simmer for 15 minutes. Add the red pepper and simmer for a further 10 minutes.

3 Blend the salt, flour, mustard and turmeric with the reserved vinegar to make a smooth paste. Stir the paste into the vegetable mixture and bring back to the boil. Simmer for 5 minutes, until the mixture has thickened. Spoon the relish into warmed sterilized jars, cover and seal. Store in a cool dark place. Use within 6 months of making.

Nutritional information per quantity: Energy 1479kcal/6291kJ; Protein 20.3g; Carbohydrate 356.7g, of which sugars 275.1g; Fat 6.4g, of which saturates 1g; Cholesterol 0mg; Calcium 307mg; Fibre 15.5g; Sodium 3085mg.

Nectarine relish

This sweet and tangy fruit relish goes very well with hot roast meats such as pork and game birds such as guinea fowl and pheasant. Make it while nectarines are plentiful and serve for Christmas.

MAKES ABOUT 450G/1LB

45ml/3 tbsp olive oil
2 Spanish (Bermuda) onions, thinly sliced
1 fresh green chilli, seeded and
  finely chopped
5ml/1 tsp finely chopped fresh rosemary
2 bay leaves
450g/1lb nectarines, stoned (pitted) and
  cut into chunks
150g/5oz/1 cup raisins
10ml/2 tsp crushed coriander seeds
350g/12oz/1½ cups demerara
  (raw) sugar
200ml/7fl oz/scant 1 cup red
  wine vinegar

1 Heat the olive oil in a large pan. Add the sliced onions, and the chopped chilli and rosemary. Add the bay leaves to the pan and cook, stirring frequently, for about 15 minutes, or until the onions have become soft.

2 Add the nectarine chunks, along with the raisins, crushed coriander seeds and demerara sugar. Pour in the red wine vinegar, then slowly bring the mixture to the boil, stirring frequently.

3 Reduce the heat and then simmer gently for 1 hour, or until the relish is thick and sticky. Stir occasionally during cooking, and more frequently towards the end of the cooking time to prevent the relish sticking to the pan.

4 Remove from the heat, then carefully spoon into warmed sterilized jars. Seal the jars, then leave them to cool completely. Store the jars in the refrigerator until ready to use. The relish will keep well in the refrigerator for up to 5 months.

Nutritional information per quantity: Energy 2408kcal/10,211kJ; Protein 16g; Carbohydrate 541.8g, of which sugars 532.6g; Fat 34.8g, of which saturates 4.7g; Cholesterol 0mg; Calcium 386mg; Fibre 14g; Sodium 127mg.

Sweet and sour pineapple relish

This simple preserve is an excellent condiment for perking up grilled chicken or bacon chops. Using canned pineapple means it can be made mainly from store-cupboard ingredients.

MAKES ABOUT 675G/1½LB

2 x 400g/14oz cans pineapple rings or
   pieces in natural juice
1 lemon
115g/4oz/½ cup sugar
45ml/3 tbsp white wine vinegar

6 spring onions (scallions),
   finely chopped
2 fresh red chillies, seeded and
   finely chopped
salt and ground black pepper

1 Drain the pineapple, reserving 120ml/4fl oz/½ cup of the juice. Pour the juice into a preserving pan. Finely chop the pineapple, if necessary, and place in a sieve (strainer) set over a bowl.

2 Pare a strip of rind from the lemon. Squeeze the lemon juice and add to the pan with the lemon rind, sugar and vinegar.

3 Cook over a low heat, stirring occasionally, until the sugar has dissolved, then bring the mixture to the boil. Cook, uncovered, over a medium heat for about 10 minutes, or until the sauce has thickened slightly.

4 Add the chopped spring onions and chillies to the pan, together with any juice that has been drained from the chopped pineapple.

5 Cook the sauce for 5 minutes, until thick and syrupy, stirring frequently towards the end of the cooking time.

6 Increase the heat slightly, add the pineapple and cook for about 4 minutes, or until most of the liquid has evaporated. Season.

7 Spoon the relish into warmed sterilized jars, cover and seal. Store in the refrigerator and eat within 3 months of making.

Nutritional information per quantity: Energy 2408kcal/10,211kJ; Protein 16g; Carbohydrate 541.8g, of which sugars 532.6g; Fat 34.8g, of which saturates 4.7g; Cholesterol 0mg; Calcium 386mg; Fibre 14g; Sodium 127mg.

Sauces and mustards

No store cupboard is complete without a bottle of tangy sauce and a jar of peppery mustard for serving with hot and cold meats, spreading over cheese on toast, or smearing in a sandwich for an extra-spicy bite. Mustard is also indispensable for enlivening mild sauces and dressings.

Roasted red pepper and chilli ketchup

Roasting the peppers gives this ketchup a richer, smoky flavour. You can add fewer or more chillies according to taste. Once opened, store in the refrigerator and use within 3 months.

**MAKES ABOUT 600ML/
1 PINT/2½ CUPS**

900g/2lb red (bell) peppers
225g/8oz shallots
1 tart cooking apple, quartered, cored and
  roughly chopped
4 fresh red chillies, seeded and chopped
1 large sprig each thyme and parsley
1 bay leaf
5ml/1 tsp coriander seeds
5ml/1 tsp black peppercorns
600ml/1 pint/2½ cups water
350ml/12fl oz/1½ cups red wine vinegar
50g/2oz/scant ¼ cup sugar
5ml/1 tsp salt
7.5ml/1½ tsp arrowroot

1 Preheat the grill (broiler). Place the peppers on a baking sheet and grill for 10–12 minutes, turning regularly, until the skins have blackened. Put the peppers in a plastic bag and leave for 5 minutes.

2 When the peppers are cool enough to handle, peel away the skin, then quarter the peppers and remove the seeds. Roughly chop the flesh and place in a large pan.

3 Put the shallots in a bowl, pour over boiling water and leave to stand for 3 minutes.

4 Drain the shallots then rinse under cold water and peel, chop and add to the pan with the apple and chillies.

5 Tie the thyme, parsley, bay leaf, coriander seeds and peppercorns in a square of muslin (cheesecloth). Add the bag of herbs and the water to the pan and bring to the boil. Reduce the heat, cover and simmer for 30 minutes. Leave to cool for 15 minutes, then remove and discard the muslin bag.

6 Purée the mixture in a food processor, then press through a sieve (strainer) and return the purée to the cleaned pan. Reserve 15ml/1 tbsp of the vinegar and add the rest to the pan with the sugar and salt.

7 Bring to the boil, stirring until the sugar has dissolved, then simmer for 45 minutes, or until the sauce is well reduced. Blend the arrowroot with the reserved vinegar, stir into the sauce, then simmer for 2–3 minutes, or until slightly thickened. Remove from the heat, then pour the sauce into hot sterilized bottles. Seal, heat treat (see page 205) and store in a cool, dark place. Use within 18 months.

Nutritional information per quantity: Energy 553kcal/2341kJ; Protein 12.8g; Carbohydrate 123.2g, of which sugars 120.5g; Fat 4.1g, of which saturates 0.9g; Cholesterol 0mg; Calcium 155mg; Fibre 18.6g; Sodium 1045mg.

Barbecue sauce

As well as enlivening burgers and other food cooked on the barbecue, this sauce is also very good for all manner of grilled meats and savoury pastries.

**MAKES ABOUT 900ML/
1½ PINTS/3¾ CUPS**

30ml/2 tbsp olive oil
1 large onion, chopped
1 garlic clove, crushed
1 fresh red chilli, seeded and sliced
2 celery sticks, sliced
1 large carrot, sliced
1 medium cooking apple, quartered,
    cored, peeled and chopped
450g/1lb ripe tomatoes, quartered
2.5ml/½ tsp ground ginger
150ml/¼ pint/⅔ cup malt vinegar
1 bay leaf
4 whole cloves
4 black peppercorns
50g/2oz/¼ cup soft light brown sugar
10ml/2 tsp English mustard
2.5ml/½ tsp salt

1 Heat the oil in a large heavy pan. Add the onion and cook over a low heat for 5 minutes.

2 Stir the crushed garlic into the onion, along with the sliced chilli, celery and carrot, and then cook for 5 minutes, stirring frequently, until the onion just begins to colour.

3 Add the apple, tomatoes, ground ginger and malt vinegar to the pan and stir to combine.

4 Put the bay leaf, whole cloves and black peppercorns on a square of muslin (cheesecloth) and tie them into a bag with fine string. Add the bag to the pan and bring to the boil. Reduce the heat, then cover the pan and simmer for about 45 minutes, stirring occasionally.

5 Add the sugar, mustard and the salt to the pan and stir until the sugar dissolves. Simmer for 5 minutes.

6 Remove the pan from the heat and then leave the mixture to cool for 10 minutes. Remove the muslin bag and discard. Press the mixture through a sieve (strainer) and return to the cleaned pan. Simmer for 10 minutes, or until thickened. Adjust the seasoning.

7 Remove the pan from the heat, then pour the sauce into hot sterilized bottles or jars. Seal the bottles or jars. then heat treat and cool. If you are using cork-topped bottles, dip the corks in wax. Store in a cool, dark place and use within 1 year. Once opened, store in the refrigerator and use within 2 months.

Nutritional information per quantity: Energy 561kcal/2359kJ; Protein 5.8g; Carbohydrate 84.3g, of which sugars 82.4g; Fat 24.7g, of which saturates 3.7g; Cholesterol 0mg; Calcium 126mg; Fibre 8.9g; Sodium 396mg.

Mint sauce

In England, mint sauce is the traditional and inseparable accompaniment to roast lamb. Its fresh, tart, astringent flavour is the perfect foil to the rich, strongly flavoured lamb.

MAKES ABOUT 250ML/8FL OZ/1 CUP

1 large bunch mint
105ml/7 tbsp boiling water
150ml/¼ pint/²/₃ cup wine vinegar
30ml/2 tbsp sugar

1 Using a sharp knife, chop the mint very finely and then place it in a 600ml/1-pint/2½-cup jug (pitcher).

2 Pour the boiling water over the mint and then leave it to infuse for about 10 minutes.

3 When the mint infusion has cooled until it has reach a lukewarm temperature, stir in the wine vinegar.

4 Add the sugar, then continue stirring the mixture (but do not mash up the mint leaves) until the sugar has dissolved completely.

5 Carefully pour the mint sauce into a sterilized bottle or jar, then seal the jar and store it in the refrigerator. The mint sauce will keep for up to 6 months stored in the refrigerator, but it is best used within 3 weeks.

Nutritional information per quantity: Energy 161kcal/685kJ; Protein 3.9g; Carbohydrate 36.6g, of which sugars 31.3g; Fat 0.7g, of which saturates 0g; Cholesterol 0mg; Calcium 226mg; Fibre 0g; Sodium 17mg.

Horseradish sauce

Fiery horseradish sauce is essential with roast beef and delicious served with smoked salmon. It is powerful so take care when handling it and wash your hands straight afterwards.

MAKES ABOUT 200ML/7FL OZ/SCANT 1 CUP

45ml/3 tbsp horseradish root
15ml/1 tbsp white wine vinegar
5ml/1 tsp sugar
pinch of salt
150ml/¼ pint/²/₃ cup thick double (heavy) cream, for serving

1 First peel the horseradish root and then grate it finely. Horseradish is a very powerful ingredient, so take care to keep the root submerged in water while you peel it. If possible, use a food processor to do the fine grating, and avert your head when removing the lid. Place the grated horseradish in a bowl, then wash your hands.

2 Add the white wine vinegar to the bowl, along with the sugar and just a pinch of salt. Stir the ingredients together until thoroughly combined.

3 Pour the mixture into a sterilized jar. It will keep in the refrigerator for up to 6 months. A few hours before serving the sauce, stir in the cream and leave it to infuse.

Nutritional information per quantity: Energy 774kcal/3190kJ; Protein 2.8g; Carbohydrate 9.9g, of which sugars 9.8g; Fat 80.7g, of which saturates 50.1g; Cholesterol 206mg; Calcium 98mg; Fibre 1.1g; Sodium 40mg.

Cumberland sauce

This sauce is thought to have been named after the Duke of Cumberland who became ruler of Hanover at a time when fruit sauces were served with meat and game in Germany. It goes well with cold cuts, pâtés and terrines, and with Christmas or Thanksgiving turkey.

**MAKES ABOUT 750ML/
1 1/4 PINTS/3 CUPS**

4 oranges
2 lemons
450g/1lb redcurrant or rowan jelly
150ml/1/4 pint/2/3 cup port
20ml/4 tsp cornflour (cornstarch)
pinch of ground ginger

1 Scrub the oranges and lemons, then remove the rind thinly, paring away any white pith.

2 Cut the orange and lemon rind into thin matchstick strips. Put the strips in a heavy pan, cover them with cold water and bring the water to the boil.

3 Simmer the rind for 2 minutes, then drain, cover with cold water, bring to the boil and simmer for about 3 minutes. Drain well and return the rind to the pan.

4 Squeeze the juice from the fruits, then add it to the pan with the redcurrant or rowan jelly. Reserve 30ml/2 tbsp of the port and add the rest to the pan.

5 Slowly bring the mixture to the boil, stirring until the jelly has melted. Simmer for 10 minutes until slightly thickened. Blend the cornflour and ginger with the reserved port and stir into the sauce. Cook over a low heat, stirring until the sauce thickens and boils. Simmer for 2 minutes.

6 Leave the sauce to cool for about 5 minutes, then stir again briefly. Remove the pan from the heat, then pour the sauce into warmed sterilized wide-necked bottles or jars, cover and seal. The sauce will keep for several weeks in the refrigerator or, if heat treated, for 6 months. Once opened, store in the refrigerator and use within 3 weeks.

Nutritional information per quantity: Energy 1481kcal/6297kJ; Protein 3g; Carbohydrate 346.9g, of which sugars 328.5g; Fat 0.1g, of which saturates 0g; Cholesterol 0mg; Calcium 63mg; Fibre 0g; Sodium 147mg.

Sherried plum sauce

Here, plums are cooked with their skins, then strained to make a smooth sauce.
Sharp cooking plums, damsons or bullaces give the best flavour and help counteract
the sweetness of the sauce, which is wonderful served with roast duck or goose.

MAKES ABOUT 400ML/
14FL OZ/1²⁄₃ CUPS

450g/1lb dark plums or damsons
125ml/4fl oz/¹⁄₂ cup dry sherry, plus
    extra to top up
30ml/2 tbsp sherry vinegar
175g/6oz/scant 1 cup light muscovado
    (brown) sugar
1 garlic clove, crushed
1.5ml/¹⁄₄ tsp salt
2.5cm/1in piece fresh root ginger, finely
    chopped
3–4 drops of Tabasco sauce

1 Cut each plum in half, then twist
the halves apart and remove the
stone (pit).

2 Roughly chop the plum flesh
and then put it in a large, heavy
pan. If you're using damsons or
bullaces, you may find it easier
simply to chop them, leaving in the
stones. Stir in the sherry and the
sherry vinegar.

3 Bring to the boil, then cover and
cook over a gentle heat for 10
minutes, or until the plums are soft.
Push the fruit through a food mill or
sieve (strainer) to remove the skins.

4 Return the purée to the pan and
add the muscovado sugar, crushed
garlic, the salt and the chopped
ginger. Stir until the sugar has
dissolved, then bring back to the
boil and simmer, uncovered, for
about 15 minutes, until thickened.

5 Remove from the heat and stir
in the Tabasco sauce. Ladle the
sauce into hot sterilized jars.
Add 5–10ml/1–2 tsp sherry
to the top of each jar, then
cover and seal. This plum
sauce will keep for several
weeks in the refrigerator or,
if heat treated (see page 205),
for 6 months. Once opened,
store in the refrigerator and
use within 3 weeks.

Nutritional information per quantity: Energy 996kcal/4237kJ; Protein 4.2g; Carbohydrate 225g, of which sugars
224.2g; Fat 0.5g, of which saturates 0g; Cholesterol 0mg; Calcium 161mg; Fibre 7.4g; Sodium 1014mg.

Aromatic mustard powder

This pungent condiment has the added flavour of herbs and spices and should be served in small quantities with meats and cheese. To serve, simply mix it with a little water.

MAKES ABOUT 200G/7OZ/ 1²/₃ CUPS

115g/4oz/1 cup mustard powder
25ml/1¹/₂ tbsp ground sea salt
5ml/1 tsp dried thyme
5ml/1 tsp dried tarragon
5ml/1 tsp mixed spice (apple pie spice)
2.5ml/¹/₂ tsp ground black pepper
2.5ml/¹/₂ tsp garlic powder (optional)

1 Put the mustard powder and sea salt in a bowl and stir together until they are evenly blended.

2 Add the dried thyme, tarragon, mixed spice and ground black pepper and the garlic powder, if using, to the mustard. Stir the mixture together well until it is thoroughly combined.

3 Carefully spoon into small, clean, dry jars, then seal tightly. Store in a cool, dark place and use the mustard powder within 6 months. (Although the mustard powder won't go off, the potency of the herbs and spices will fade with age and the final mustard will not have the same lovely, strong flavour.)

4 To serve, prepare the mustard about 10 minutes before needed. It is best when freshly made, so mix up small quantities as and when you need it. Transfer the desired quantity of mustard powder to a small serving bowl, add an equal amount of cold water and mix well until smooth.

Nutritional information per quantity:
Energy 520kcal/2167kJ; Protein 33.2g; Carbohydrate 23.8g, of which sugars 0g; Fat 51.9g, of which saturates 1.7g; Cholesterol 5mg; Calcium 381mg; Fibre 0g; Sodium 5901mg.

Tomato ketchup

Sweet, tangy, spicy tomato ketchup is perfect for serving with barbecued or grilled burgers and sausages. This home-made variety is so much better than store-bought tomato ketchup.

MAKES ABOUT 1.3KG/3LB

2.25kg/5lb very ripe tomatoes
1 onion
6 cloves
4 allspice berries
6 black peppercorns
1 fresh rosemary sprig
25g/1oz fresh root ginger, sliced
1 celery heart
30ml/2 tbsp soft light brown sugar
65ml/4¹/₂ tbsp raspberry vinegar
3 garlic cloves, peeled
15ml/1 tbsp salt

1 Peel and seed the tomatoes, then chop the flesh and place in a pan.

2 Peel the onion, leaving the tip and root intact and stud it with the cloves.

3 Put the onion into a double layer of muslin (cheesecloth) with the allspice berries, black peppercorns, rosemary sprig and sliced root ginger. Tie them together, then add the bag to the pan.

4 Roughly chop the celery, including the leaves. Add to the pan with the sugar, vinegar, garlic and salt.

5 Bring the mixture to the boil over a fairly high heat, stirring occasionally. Reduce the heat, and simmer for 1¹/₂–2 hours, stirring regularly to prevent it sticking, until reduced by half.

6 Remove from the heat, purée the mixture in a food processor, then return to the pan. Bring to the boil and simmer for 15 minutes.

7 Remove the mixture from the heat again, bottle in clean, sterilized jars and then store in the refrigerator. Use within 2 weeks.

Nutritional information per quantity:
Energy 543kcal/2327kJ; Protein 18.1g;
Carbohydrate 108.5g, of which sugars 107.2g;
Fat 7.5g, of which saturates 2.3g; Cholesterol 0mg;
Calcium 313mg; Fibre 26.6g; Sodium 6281mg.

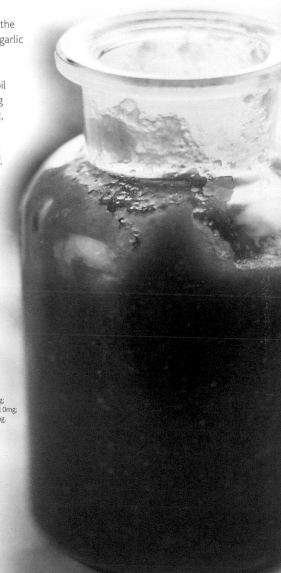

Moutarde aux fines herbes

This fragrant mustard may be used as a tasty condiment or for coating meats such as chicken and pork before cooking.

MAKES ABOUT 300ML/1/2 PINT/11/4 CUPS

75g/3oz/scant 1/2 cup white mustard seeds
50g/2oz/1/4 cup soft light brown sugar
5ml/1 tsp salt
5ml/1 tsp whole peppercorns
2.5ml/1/2 tsp ground turmeric
200ml/7fl oz/scant 1 cup distilled malt vinegar
60ml/4 tbsp chopped fresh mixed herbs, such as parsley, sage, thyme and rosemary

1 Put the mustard seeds, sugar, salt, whole peppercorns and ground turmeric into a food processor or blender and process for about 1 minute, or until the peppercorns are coarsely chopped.

2 Gradually add the vinegar to the mustard mixture, 15ml/1 tbsp at a time, processing well between each addition, then continue processing until a coarse paste forms.

3 Add the chopped fresh herbs to the mustard and mix well, then leave to stand for 10–15 minutes until the mustard thickens slightly.

4 Spoon the mustard into a 300ml/1/2-pint/11/4-cup sterilized jar. Cover the surface of the mustard with a baking parchment disc, then seal with a screw-top lid or a cork, and label. Store in a cool, dark place.

Nutritional information per quantity: Energy 553kcal/2324kJ; Protein 23.4g; Carbohydrate 69.1g, of which sugars 53.4g; Fat 34.5g, of which saturates 1.1g; Cholesterol 3mg; Calcium 374mg; Fibre 2.5g; Sodium 23mg.

Honey and cinnamon mustard

Home-made mustards mature to make the most aromatic of condiments. This honey mustard is wonderful served with meats and cheeses.

MAKES ABOUT 500G/11/4LB

225g/8oz/1 cup mustard seeds
15ml/1 tbsp ground cinnamon
2.5ml/1/2 tsp ground ginger
300ml/1/2 pint/11/4 cups white wine vinegar
90ml/6 tbsp dark clear honey (this recipe needs well-flavoured, clear, runny honey – set (crystallized) honey does not have the right consistency and will not work well)

1 Put the mustard seeds in a bowl with the ground cinnamon and ginger. Now pour over the white wine vinegar. Stir the mixture together well, then leave it to soak overnight.

2 The next day, transfer the mustard mixture to a mortar and then pound it with a pestle. While you are pounding the mixture, pour in the honey very gradually in a slow, steady stream.

3 Continue pounding and mixing until the mustard resembles a stiff paste. If the mixture is too stiff, add a little extra white wine vinegar in order to achieve the desired consistency.

4 Carefully spoon the mustard into four sterilized jars, then seal and label them. Store the jars in the refrigerator and use the mustard within 4 weeks.

Nutritional information per quantity: Energy 1276kcal/5345kJ; Protein 65.4g; Carbohydrate 115.3g, of which sugars 68.8g; Fat 101.5g, of which saturates 3.4g; Cholesterol 9mg; Calcium 747mg; Fibre 0g; Sodium 21mg.

Clove-spiced mustard

This spicy mustard is the perfect accompaniment to robust red meats such as sausages and steaks, particularly when they are cooked on the barbecue.

**MAKES ABOUT 300ML/
¹⁄₂ PINT/1¹⁄₄ CUPS**

**75g/3oz/scant ¹⁄₂ cup white
    mustard seeds**
50g/2oz/¹⁄₄ cup soft light brown sugar
5ml/1 tsp salt
5ml/1 tsp black peppercorns
**5ml/1 tsp whole cloves (try to avoid
    using ground cloves – they have less
    flavour)**
5ml/1 tsp turmeric
**200ml/7fl oz/scant 1 cup distilled
    malt vinegar**

1 Put the white mustard seeds, light brown sugar, salt, black peppercorns, cloves and turmeric into a food processor or blender and process.

2 Gradually pour in the malt vinegar, 15ml/1 tbsp at a time, processing well between each addition. Continue processing the spiced mixture until it forms a fairly thick, coarse paste.

3 Leave the mustard to stand for 10–15 minutes until it has thickened slightly in consistency.

4 Spoon the mixture into a 300ml/¹⁄₂-pint/1¹⁄₄-cup sterilized jar, or several smaller jars, using a funnel. Cover the surface with a baking parchment disc, then seal with a screw-top lid or a cork, and label.

Nutritional information per quantity: Energy 536kcal/2254kJ; Protein 21.9g; Carbohydrate 67.8g, of which sugars 52.2g; Fat 33.8g, of which saturates 1.1g; Cholesterol 3mg; Calcium 275mg; Fibre 0g; Sodium 1972mg.

Spiced tamarind mustard

Tamarind has a distinctive sweet-and-sour flavour, a dark brown colour and sticky texture. Combined with spices and ground mustard seeds, it makes a wonderful condiment.

MAKES ABOUT 200G/7OZ

115g/4oz tamarind block
150ml/¼ pint/⅔ cup warm water
50g/2oz/¼ cup yellow mustard seeds
25ml/1½ tbsp black or brown
   mustard seeds
10ml/2 tsp clear honey
pinch of ground cardamom
pinch of salt

1 Put the tamarind block in a small bowl and then pour over the warm water. Leave the tamarind to soak for 30 minutes, then mash it to a pulp with a fork. Strain it through a fine sieve (strainer) into a bowl.

2 Grind all the mustard seeds in a spice mill or coffee grinder, then add them to the tamarind.

3 Now add the honey, ground cardamom and the salt. Spoon the mixture into sterilized jars, then cover and seal them. The mustard will be ready to eat in 3–4 days. Store the tamarind mustard in a cool, dark place and use it within 4 months.

Nutritional information per quantity: Energy 376kcal/1570kJ; Protein 22.3g; Carbohydrate 24.2g, of which sugars 8.7g; Fat 34.1g, of which saturates 1.1g; Cholesterol 3mg; Calcium 295mg; Fibre 1.3g; Sodium 74mg.

Tarragon and champagne mustard

This delicately flavoured mustard is well worth making and goes particularly well with cold chicken, fish and shellfish.

MAKES ABOUT 250G/9OZ

30ml/2 tbsp mustard seeds
75ml/5 tbsp champagne vinegar
115g/4oz/1 cup mustard powder
115g/4oz/1/2 cup soft light brown sugar
2.5ml/1/2 tsp salt
50ml/2fl oz virgin olive oil
60ml/4 tbsp chopped fresh tarragon

1 Put the mustard seeds and champagne vinegar in a bowl and then leave to soak overnight.

2 The next day, tip the mustard seeds and vinegar into a food processor and add the mustard powder, light brown sugar and the salt.

3 Blend the mustard mixture until smooth, then slowly pour in the olive oil in a steady stream while continuing to blend.

4 Tip the mustard into a bowl, stir in the chopped fresh tarragon, then spoon the mixture into sterilized jars. Seal the jars and store them in a cool, dark place until you are ready to use them.

Nutritional information per quantity: Energy 1405kcal/5885kJ; Protein 42.5g; Carbohydrate 150.2g, of which sugars 120.2g; Fat 98.4g, of which saturates 6.9g; Cholesterol 6mg; Calcium 539mg; Fibre 0g; Sodium 14mg.

Tangy horseradish mustard

This mustard has a wonderfully creamy, peppery taste and is delicious spread thinly inside cold roast beef sandwiches.

MAKES ABOUT 400G/14OZ

25ml/1 1/2 tbsp mustard seeds
250ml/8fl oz/1 cup boiling water
115g/4oz/1 cup mustard powder
115g/4oz/scant 1/2 cup sugar
120ml/4fl oz/1/2 cup white wine vinegar or cider vinegar
50ml/2fl oz/1/4 cup olive oil
5ml/1 tsp lemon juice
30ml/2 tbsp horseradish sauce (home-made if possible)

1 Put the mustard seeds in a bowl and pour over the boiling water. Set aside and then leave to soak for at least 1 hour.

2 Drain the mustard seeds and discard the soaking liquid, then tip the seeds into a food processor or blender.

3 Add the mustard powder, sugar, white wine or cider vinegar, olive oil, lemon juice and horseradish sauce to the mustard-seed mixture.

4 Process the ingredients into a smooth paste, then spoon the mustard into sterilized jars. Store the mustard in the refrigerator and use within 3 months.

Nutritional information per quantity: Energy 1428kcal/5982kJ; Protein 41.8g; Carbohydrate 154.5g, of which sugars 124.7g; Fat 98.6g, of which saturates 7.1g; Cholesterol 10mg; Calcium 536mg; Fibre 0.8g; Sodium 287mg.

Ingredients and techniques

From jewel-like jams and jellies to

sweet fruits preserved in sugar syrups

and alcohol, and from spicy chutneys

and relishes to tart sauces and pickles,

this easy-to-follow guide leads you

through all the classic ingredients

and the key preserving techniques,

offering advice on how to avoid the

potential pitfalls.

Soft fruits and berries

These delicate fruits are the epitome of summer and early autumn and can be made into wonderful jams and jellies. Despite their distinctive flavours and appearance, many are interchangeable in recipes.

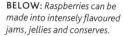

BELOW: *Raspberries can be made into intensely flavoured jams, jellies and conserves.*

BELOW: *Tiny redcurrants have a distinctive, tart flavour and are particularly good made into sparkling jellies.*

STRAWBERRIES

These fruits are one of the most popular berries for jam-making and have a wonderfully fragrant flavour. Choose medium-size berries with an intense fragrance because these will give the preserve a good fruity flavour. Look for just-ripe, firm, fresh berries and use them for jam-making as soon as possible after picking, because this is when the pectin content is highest. Rinse them only if absolutely necessary; if you do wash them, don't cut or hull them beforehand, or water will penetrate the fruit.

Tiny wild strawberries (*fraises de bois*), which are also known as alpine strawberries, have a pungent aroma and flavour and can be used whole in conserves.

THE RASPBERRY AND BLACKBERRY FAMILY

Technically, each berry is composed of multiple fruits because every tiny segment contains a hard seed. Jams made from these fruits have a high seed content, so are often strained and made into seedless jams or jellies. The true raspberry is a bright crimson colour; yellow and white raspberries are also available and these have a deliciously delicate flavour, but make less attractive preserves.

Blackberries are related to the raspberry. They are a wild fruit, native to Europe and the United States. They are now grown commercially to produce larger, juicier berries. Blackberries contain sufficient pectin to make intensely flavoured jellies, and go extremely well with apples. This classic combination originally came about because early ripening apples were scarce and wild blackberries could be used to make them go further.

Dewberries are closely related to the blackberry and are similar in appearance. Cloudberries, which grow in North America and Canada, are a bright orange-red colour; the Scandinavian (or Arctic) cloudberry, which also grows in Scotland, is a pinky yellow colour with an almost caramel flavour. Loganberries (a cross between the raspberry and the Pacific blackberry) look like elongated, very dark raspberries but have a juicier, fuller flavour. Tayberries are a similar hybrid and are large, conical and deep purple. Boysenberries are long, dark red berries with a sharp flavour. All these berries can be successfully preserved in the same way as raspberries and blackberries.

RIGHT: *Strawberries are one of the most popular fruits for jam-making.*

CURRANTS

These come in black, red and white varieties. They have a sharp, intense flavour and are picked in bunches on stems. Blackcurrants and redcurrants are most common.

Whitecurrants are an albino strain of redcurrants and have a less acidic flavour. Currants are high in both pectin and acid, and need little cooking. Blackcurrants are usually made into jam, and red- and whitecurrants into jelly. The simplest way to remove currants from the stalk is to run the prongs of a fork gently down the stalk over a bowl.

BLUEBERRIES AND BILBERRIES

These are small, dark-coloured fruits that grow wild in Britain, Europe and the United States.

Bilberries, the European species, are dark bluish black with a soft bloom. The slightly flattened sphere-shaped berries measure no more than 1cm/½in across.

The larger cultivated blueberry and the wild huckleberry have a similar appearance but a sweeter flavour.

CRANBERRIES

Small, hard, shiny, deep-red cranberries are a member of the blueberry and bilberry family. They are much too sour to eat raw but, once cooked with sugar, can be transformed into sparkling bright-red jellies and rich, jam-like sauces, which are traditionally served with turkey.

GOOSEBERRIES

These are popular in northern Europe, but are rarely eaten in other parts of the world. Most bushes produce hard oval berries, dark green in colour with paler stripes, and a smooth or, more usually, fuzzy skin. There is also a softer, pale purple variety.

The fruit is usually too sour to eat raw, but can be made into very good jellies, jams, chutneys and relishes. Gooseberries are rich in pectin, especially when slightly unripe,

so they produce jams and jellies with a good set. Unless the gooseberry mixture is being strained or sieved, the fruits should always be "topped and tailed" (trimmed) before preserving.

PHYSALIS

These attractive fruits are also known as Cape gooseberries, although they are unrelated to gooseberries. The golden berries are enclosed in an inedible papery husk. Physalis make good, if rather expensive, jams and bottled fruits.

Hedgerow fruits

Elderberries are the fruit of elderberry trees, which grow all over Europe, West Asia and the United States. The berries are small and very dark bluish black and hang in umbrella-like clusters. They can be stripped from the sprigs with a fork and are excellent preserved with crab apples or cooking apples.

Haws are the small dark berries of the hawthorn or May tree. They are slightly astringent and very good cooked with apples to make a dark red jelly.

Hips or rosehips are the orangey-red seedpods of the rose and can be made into a bittersweet jelly.

Sloes, a type of plum, are the fruit of the blackthorn bush, which is found in Europe and West Asia. The fruits are black with a blue bloom, and measure only about 1cm/½in across. They can be combined with apples and made into a fragrant jelly.

BELOW: *Blueberries have a mild, fragrant flavour and can be made into richly coloured jams.*

Orchard fruits

Apples and pears, which are available all year round, are the most common members of this family of fruits. They can be made into jams, jellies and chutneys, bottled in syrup or dried into chewy rings. Other, more unusual, orchard fruits include quinces, japonicas and medlars.

APPLES

There are thousands of varieties of apples, although choice in the shops is usually limited to just a few. Among the most popular eating apples are Gala, Russet, Granny Smith, Braeburn, Golden Delicious and Cox's Orange Pippin. These all have their own flavours, which are are captured when the apples are bottled in spiced or flavoured syrup. Well-flavoured eating apples may also be used in chutneys and relishes when retaining the texture of the fruit is desirable.

Cooking apples are more frequently used in preserves and give a good pulpy texture to chutneys.

Apples are high in pectin and, on their own, produce rather bland, colourless jams, so they are often combined with fruits that have a good flavour and low pectin content to produce a jam or jelly with a better set. Most of the pectin in apples is in the skin and seeds, so peelings and cores are often used to make a pectin stock. This is then stirred into other fruit jams and jellies to improve their set, without affecting their flavour.

CRAB APPLES

These small apples can be gathered from the wild, from cultivated garden trees. They have a sharp, rich flavour and are very good used on their own or combined with other hedgerow fruits.

PEARS

Unlike apples, pears are low in pectin, so are less frequently used in jams and jellies. Their sweet, mild flavour and tender texture make them popular for chutneys and they are superb preserved in syrup or alcohol, or pickled in raspberry vinegar, either whole, halved or quartered. The British Conference and the American Bosc are particularly good for preserving.

QUINCES

Golden-yellow quinces can be the shape and size of a small pear or apple, or the size of a large pear, depending on the variety. The flesh is hard, granular and sour when eaten raw, but cooking makes it smooth and tender, with a delicate soft pink tinge and a sherbet-like aromatic flavour. Quinces are rich in pectin and can be made into jellies, fruit cheeses and butters; these may be golden or deep pink depending on the variety used.

JAPONICAS

These small, round, green fruits are also known as Japanese quinces. They can be preserved in the same ways as quinces, but have a slightly sharper, lemony flavour.

MEDLARS

These are small brown fruits with a squashed round shape and an open end revealing the seeds. The flesh is very hard and mouth-puckeringly acidic when first picked. To soften and sweeten the fruit, it must be "bletted" or allowed to ferment slightly. The flesh is dry and sticky and tastes like the flesh of dried dates. A mixture of unripe and "bletted" medlars can be made into aromatic preserves such as jams, jellies and cheeses.

BELOW: *Quinces have a distinctive, aromatic flavour and can be made into delicious jellies, which are good spread on bread or toast.*

Stone fruits

These are all fruits of the prunus genus, recognized by their single central woody stone (pit), soft flesh and thin skin. They are well-suited to jam-making and can also be used whole or halved in bottled preserves. These fruits come in a wide variety of colours, textures and flavours, from tender pale-orange apricots and yellow-skinned tart plums, to glossy sweet red cherries, and they can be made into numerous types of preserves.

PLUMS

These fruits range in colour from pale gold through red and crimson to deep purple. When buying, choose firm, unwrinkled fruits that still have a slight bloom. They will keep for several days at room temperature, but will continue to ripen. Once they are almost ripe, they can be stored in the refrigerator for a few more days. Use them when just ripe to make richly flavoured jams.

Greengages are small, green, fragrant plums. They are primarily dessert fruits, but also good bottled or made into luxurious jams.

Purple-black damsons are available only in the early autumn months. These fruits are small and have a sour taste. They make superb jams and excellent damson cheese.

Bullaces are small, round plums that grow wild throughout Europe and can be used in the same way as damsons.

CHERRIES

These fruits are divided into two main groups: sweet cherries, which may be black (actually deep red) or white (usually yellow), and sour cherries, of which the best known are Morellos. When buying, the cherry's stem is a good indicator of freshness – it should be green and flexible not brown and brittle. Avoid any fruit that is overly soft or split. Cherries are low in pectin, so must either be combined with apples or other pectin-rich fruit, or commercial or home-made pectin stock needs to be added when making jam or other set preserves. Both sweet and sour cherries are excellent pickled or bottled.

PEACHES AND NECTARINES

A good peach or nectarine will be richly coloured and heavy, with a strong aroma.

BELOW: *Plums are most plentiful in the summer, so it is well worth making a batch of jam to enjoy during the rest of the year.*

ABOVE: *Sweet black cherries can be made into the most delicious, richly flavoured preserves.*

Peaches have downy skins and the most common types have yellow or pink flesh. The white-fleshed and pale-skinned variety is the sweetest of all.

Nectarines are similar to peaches but they have smooth and shiny skins and a slightly sharper taste – like a cross between a peach and a plum.

These fruits make great jams, are good pickled or bottled, and are also excellent made into fruity chutneys. They should be skinned before using in jams and chutneys.

APRICOTS

With their slightly sweet-and-sour flavour, soft texture and downy skins, apricots are delicious eaten fresh and raw. Cooking with sugar intensifies their flavour. Slightly under-ripe apricots can be poached in a sugar syrup with a dash of lime juice and bottled. Just-ripe fruits can be cooked with sugar to make jams. Apricots and almonds are a popular combination. Try adding split almonds to conserves for extra flavour and texture. Choose apricots with the strongest colour for the sweetest flavour.

Citrus fruits

With their aromatic acidity, citrus fruits are the main ingredient of nearly all marmalades and fruit curds. They are also often added to other preserves because they have a high pectin and acid content, and they are frequently used in jams and jellies to help achieve a good set. The pungency and sharpness of citrus fruit not only adds flavour but also offsets sweetness.

Members of the citrus family include lemons, limes, oranges, grapefruits and tangerines as well as the more exotic Ugli fruit, citrons and kumquats, and hybrids such as the clementine and the limequat.

ABOVE: *Sweet, juicy oranges are most commonly preserved as tangy breakfast marmalades and orange curds.*

ORANGES

There are three types of sweet orange: the common orange is a medium-size fruit with a fine-grained skin, and popular varieties are Valencia and Jaffa, and Shamouti, which is available only in the winter. These are the juiciest oranges and are ideal for sweet marmalades and orange curds. They often contain a lot of pips (seeds), which are essential for making marmalade because they are high in pectin and help the marmalade to set.

Navel oranges are seedless, so are better preserved whole, in segments or in slices. Red-flushed blood oranges have ruby-coloured flesh and a rich, almost berry-like flavour. These oranges make excellent marmalades when combined with sharper lemons, but are less successful for making curd because their deeply coloured juice looks rather unappetizing when mixed with yellow butter and eggs.

Bitter Seville oranges have a high pectin and acid content, as well as an excellent, punchy flavour. They are considered to make the finest marmalades. (The bulk of the Spanish crop is exported to Britain for this purpose.) The Seville orange season is a fairly short one and the fruits are available for only a few weeks during the winter. However, bitter oranges can be successfully frozen whole or chopped. Alternatively, the oranges can be chopped and cooked without sugar until they are very soft before cooling and freezing. When ready to use, the frozen oranges can be thawed and then boiled with sugar until they reach setting point.

ABOVE: *Sharp, zesty lemons are widely used in both sweet and savoury preserves.*

LEMONS

In the preserving kitchen, lemons are indispensable. They add acid and pectin to jams and jellies made from low-pectin fruits, such as strawberries and peaches, which are difficult to set. Lemon juice also gives jellies a sparkling appearance. A dash of lemon juice added to preserves made from soft fruits, such as strawberries, and exotic fruits, such as papayas, helps bring out their flavour. A few spoonfuls of lemon juice added to cold water makes an acidulated dip that will prevent cut fruits, such as pears and apples, from discolouring.

Small, thin-skinned lemons are juicier, so are perfect for making curds; larger, more knobbly ones have a higher proportion of peel and pith to flesh, so are better for marmalades and crystallizing.

LIMES

These small green fruits flourish in near-tropical conditions. They have a distinctive, tangy flavour and are one of the most sour citrus fruits. A squeeze of lime juice can be added to jams and jellies instead of lemon juice to enhance the flavour of the fruit and to improve the set. It goes particularly well with tropical fruits, such as mangoes and papayas.

GRAPEFRUITS

These are among the largest citrus fruits, with a diameter of up to 15cm/6in. The flesh of grapefruits varies in colour from pale yellow to the dark reddish-pink of sweeter ruby grapefruits. The yellow-skinned and -fleshed varieties have a sharp, refreshing flavour that makes good marmalade. "Sweetie" grapefruits are less sharp: they have a vibrant, bright-green skin.

CITRONS

These large, lemon-shaped fruits grow to 20cm/8in in length. They have a fairly thick, lumpy, greenish-yellow peel that is often crystallized and is used in commercial crystallized peel. The sour-tasting pulp is sometimes made into sweet preserves, but it has no other culinary use.

POMELOS

Also known as shaddocks, these large citrus fruits resemble pear-shaped grapefruits. The flesh can be used to make jams and the rind can be crystallized with sugar or used to make marmalade.

TANGERINES AND MANDARIN ORANGES

These are the generic names for small, flat citrus fruits with loose skins and a sweet or tart-sweet flavour. Satsumas, clementines and mineolas also fall into this group. Satsumas are slightly tart and very juicy; clementines (a cross between the tangerine and the bitter orange) are similar but have a thinner, more tight-fitting skin. Mineolas are larger. They are hybrids of the grapefruit and tangerine, have a sharp, tangy flavour and resemble oranges in size and colour.

BELOW: *Tiny orange kumquats look delightful preserved in syrup.*

KUMQUATS AND LIMEQUATS

The tiny, orange, oval kumquat with its distinctive sweet-sour flavour can be eaten whole and unpeeled; the rind has a sweeter flavour than the flesh. Kumquats are delicious pickled, preserved in syrup or crystallized.

Limequats are a cross between a lime and a kumquat. The small, bright-green fruits have a fragrant flavour and can be preserved in the same way as kumquats, although they have a slightly more sour flavour. The two fruits look very pretty bottled together in the same jar and make a lovely gift.

HYBRID FRUITS

There are a huge number of citrus hybrids that are bred for flavour, colour or to be seedless.

Ugli fruit

This hybrid of the grapefruit, tangerine and orange is available in winter. It has a loose, rough, greeny-yellow skin and a slightly squashed look. It is very juicy and sweet and can be used instead of grapefruit in marmalades.

Temple oranges

These loose-skinned fruits are a cross between a tangerine and an orange. Slightly oval in shape, they have rough, thick, deep orange skin, which makes them popular for marmalade-making in the United States. The flesh is sweet, yet tart and contains a fair number of seeds. Temple oranges are in season from December to March.

Buying and storing

Look for firm, plump citrus fruits that feel heavy for their size, because this indicates that the fruit will be juicy. Avoid dry, wrinkled specimens, soft squashy fruit or any with brown spots. Green patches on lemons and yellow patches on limes are a sign of immaturity.

Citrus fruits can be kept at room temperature for several days, but for longer storage, keep them in the refrigerator, putting unwaxed fruits in a plastic bag. Always wash and scrub citrus fruits before using them in preserves.

Tropical fruits

With imports from many parts of the world, tropical fruits are now available all year round. They are often vibrantly coloured with fabulous flavours and make luxurious jams and chutneys.

PINEAPPLES
These distinctive fruits have juicy, sweet and refreshing golden flesh. They make lovely jams and crisp-textured relishes, ideal for serving with chicken, pork and ham. Pineapple rings are also good crystallized.

GUAVAS
These have a sweet, spicy flavour, with granular flesh that becomes creamy when ripe. Guavas make fragrant jams, cheeses and jellies. It is essential to add lemon or lime juice to guava preserves to achieve a good set.

BELOW: *Fragrant mangoes are fabulous made into sweet and tangy chutney.*

PAPAYAS
Also known as pawpaws, these pear-shaped fruits have a green skin that turns a speckled yellow when the fruit is ripe. The flesh is an orange-pink colour with a sweet flavour and perfumed aroma. Use ripe fruits to make jams and butters, and firm, slightly under-ripe fruits for chutneys.

MANGOES
The skins of these luscious fruits range in colour from green, through yellow and orange, to red. Just-ripe and green under-ripe mangoes make excellent, highly flavoured chutneys and pickles.

BANANAS
These long, yellow fruits make delicious, though not particularly attractive, jams. Bananas are also good in fruity chutneys, particularly spicy Indian-style preserves.

Dried bananas are sun-dried in their skins, then peeled to reveal dark, sticky fruit inside. They have a concentrated flavour and can add sweetness to chutneys.

KIWI FRUITS
Although completely unrelated to the gooseberry, these fuzzy, brown, egg-shaped fruits were once known as Chinese gooseberries. Kiwi fruits have a slightly sharp flavour so it is usually better to use sugar with pectin than to add lemon juice to get a good set.

PASSION FRUIT
These oval fruits have leathery, reddish-purple skins that go dimpled when ripe. Inside are small, hard, edible seeds, surrounded by fragrant, intensely flavoured orange pulp. The pulp and seeds may be scooped out of the halved shells and made into jam. Alternatively, the pulp can be rubbed through a fine sieve (strainer) with a spoonful of boiling water to extract the juice, which can then be used with other fruit to make delicious jams, jellies and curds.

TAMARILLOS
These egg-shaped fruits of the tomato family (sometimes known as "tree tomatoes") may be yellow, red, or dark red; the yellow variety has the finest flavour. Tamarillos can be used in the same way as tomatoes to make pickles and chutneys, but the skin has a very bitter taste so the fruit should be peeled; blanch the fruits first to loosen their skins.

POMEGRANATES
These are the shape and size of an orange. They have tough, leathery skin and a large calyx, and range in colour from deep yellow to crimson. Inside these fruits are dozens of white seeds surrounded by transluscent pinkish-red flesh, encased in a cream-coloured membrane. The seeds, pith and membranes are bitter so it is the juice that is extracted to make jams and jellies.

Pomegranates were among the first fruits to be cultivated and come in a vast array of shapes, sizes and colours.

Melons, grapes, dates and **figs**

These fruits don't fit into any particular category. They were among the first to be cultivated and all come in a vast array of shapes, sizes and colours.

MELONS

There are two kinds of melon: the dessert melon and the watermelon. Dessert melons may have green or yellow skins, sometimes streaky or netted (with fibrous markings), and fragrant, dense flesh, ranging from pale green to deep orange. The flavour of melon in preserves is not intense. Melons work well if combined with strong flavourings such as ginger, or other fruits such as pineapple, peach and mango. Watermelons have a high water content, at around 90 per cent, so the flesh is rarely used in preserves. The skin can be diced and pickled.

GRAPES

Of the many grape varieties that are available, the smaller seedless grapes are preferable for preserves because they need less preparation and have thin skins with little tannin. Usually, grapes are referred to as either black or white, although the colours vary a great deal from pale green to pinkish red and purplish black. Grape flavours range from honey-sweet to sharp and almost lemon-scented.

Grapes make good jams, conserves and jellies that are sometimes flavoured with alcohol such as wine. They can also be pickled or included in chutneys and relishes.

DATES

These delicious fruits are soft, plump and glossy. Fresh dates are packed with concentrated sugar. The thin, papery skins should be slipped off and the long stone (pit) removed before the flesh is added to chutneys.

The sweet flavour of dates combines very well with vinegar to make a wonderful sweet-and-sour preserve that goes particularly well with cheese. Semi-dried and dried dates are also widely available and can be added to chutneys.

ABOVE: *Juicy black grapes are good for making into delicate, fragrant, sparkling jellies.*

FIGS

These fragile fruits have thin skins that may be purple or greenish gold; inside is a glorious soft, scented flesh filled with tiny round seeds. When figs are plentiful, they can be made into luxurious conserves and delicious chutneys. Warm spices, such as cinnamon and vanilla, go very well with figs.

Dried figs, with their concentrated flavour, make a thick, dark and delicious jam. A little grated orange rind added to the mixture heightens the flavour.

RHUBARB

Technically, rhubarb is the stem of a vegetable. Outdoor-grown rhubarb is available in late spring and has crimson and green stems; forced rhubarb, cultivated indoors without light, has thin, tender, pale stems. The former can be made into chutney, the latter into a delicately flavoured jam. Rhubarb has a very sharp, intense flavour and goes particularly well with orange and ginger.

BELOW: *The orange flesh of the cantaloupe is excellent scooped into balls and preserved in a sweet syrup.*

Vegetable fruits

Sweet (bell) peppers, tomatoes and aubergines (eggplants) are fruits, but are treated like vegetables.

SWEET PEPPERS
These are the mildest members of the capsicum family. Young peppers have a sharp flavour and are bright green. As they mature, they become sweeter and turn yellow, then orange and finally red. Preserved green peppers tend to lose their colour with long-term storage, which is unimportant in dark chutneys, but best avoided in clear pickles.

CHILLIES
These small peppers with a spicy kick are the world's most popular spice. Green chillies are immature, while red

ABOVE: *Crisp green peppers are good in dark-coloured relishes.*

ABOVE: *Tomatoes have tough skins so are often better peeled before adding to pickles and preserves.*

ones are ripe. As a very general rule, chillies sweeten as they ripen, so dark-green chillies tend to be hotter than paler green ones and red ones. Heat is influenced by a combination of variety and the climate. Anaheim and Dutch chillies are mild, jalapeño and Scotch bonnets are much hotter, and tiny Thai or bird's eye chillies are very hot. Dried chillies are used in most pickling spices.

TOMATOES
From unripe green tomatoes to ripe red ones, tomatoes are used in all types of pickles and preserves. Ripe tomatoes may be yellow or red, depending on variety, and their sweetness or acidity varies according to type as well as how ripe they were when picked. The common round tomato is juicy and fairly acidic. Italian plum tomatoes have an elongated shape with denser flesh and a sweeter flavour. Tiny cherry tomatoes are very

ABOVE: *Baby aubergines are great pickled whole in brine or vinegar with whole spices.*

sweet, while beefsteak tomatoes are very large and can weigh up to 450g/ 1lb. Unripe green tomatoes are usually picked at the end of the season when there is not enough sun to ripen them. They are often made into green tomato chutney, or included in tart relishes such as piccalilli.

AUBERGINES/EGGPLANTS
The most common aubergines are large, dark purple and oval but there are also smaller round purple ones, and a little oval, ivory-white variety that inspired the American name eggplant. Aubergines may be pickled raw, either sliced or whole, but they are more usually chopped and cooked in pickles. Aubergines are often salted when making chutneys and pickles to extract some of the moisture, which would otherwise dilute the mixture. Aubergines can be stored in the refrigerator for up to two weeks before preserving.

Vegetables

Many kinds of vegetables can be preserved and made into savoury pickles and chutneys. These vegetables include onions, carrots, peas, mushrooms and squashes.

ONIONS

These include strongly flavoured brown-skinned onions, used for everyday cooking, and the larger mild, sweet and juicy Spanish (Bermuda) onions, also known as yellow onions. White onions with papery skins and red onions are mild and sweet, the latter adding a good colour to preserves. All types of onion can be made into onion chutneys and relishes, sliced and pickled in rings, or dried.

Pickling onions have brown papery skins and are also called button onions or pearl onions. The milder-tasting and smaller silverskin onions can also be pickled.

SHALLOTS

These are a different variety of onion, which are grown in clusters rather than as single bulbs. Shallots have a fuller, sweeter flavour than onions and are delicious pickled.

SPRING ONIONS

Also known as green onions or scallions, these are young bulb onions. Long cooking does not suit spring onions, so they are rarely used in chutneys. They may, however, be added to relishes with shorter cooking times.

LEEKS

Long, thin leeks are the mildest members of the onion family. They are included in chutneys to add texture and flavour, or pickled on their own.

GARLIC

This is the most pungent member of the onion family. One or two cloves can be used to add a subtle flavour to chutney and relishes. Vinegar can be flavoured with garlic, then used to make preserves; peel the cloves and add 5–6 to each 600ml/1 pint/2$\frac{1}{2}$ cups vinegar. Leave for 2 weeks to infuse. Use within 4 months.

MUSHROOMS

There are dozens of edible mushrooms. The common cultivated mushroom is sold at various stages in its growth. Button (white) mushrooms are the youngest and these are the best for pickling and preserving. When the cap has partially opened, mushrooms are sold as cup mushrooms and, when opened out completely, as flat or Portabello mushrooms. Mushroom varieties such as pale, fan-shaped oyster and dark brown, cup-shaped shiitake are less suitable for preserves because they lose their delicate texture and become rubbery.

Mushrooms are often flavoured with herbs such as dill, and warm spices such as mace. Mushrooms can also be dried successfully – shiitake mushrooms and wild fungi dry particularly well.

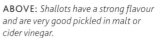

ABOVE: *Shallots have a strong flavour and are very good pickled in malt or cider vinegar.*

BEETROOT/BEET

Dark ruby-red beetroot has a rich, earthy, sweet flavour and is one of the most commonly preserved root vegetables. Pickled beetroot is eaten throughout Europe, and sweet-and-sour Harvard beets are popular in the United States. There are two varieties of beetroot: globe and a long, slender variety. The former is usually preserved whole and the latter sliced into rounds.

CARROTS

These sweet-tasting orange roots can be chopped or grated and used in chutneys, relishes and wonderful sweet jams.

PARSNIPS

These are closely related to the carrot, but with a sweeter taste. They should be scrubbed before preserving and peeled if they are tough. Try to use young vegetables because large roots can be woody.

SWEDES/RUTABAGAS

The globe-shaped swede has creamy orange flesh and a delicate, slightly sweet flavour.

TURNIPS

These are smaller than swedes. They have a smoother skin and white flesh with a peppery flavour.

CELERIAC

This knobbly root is related to celery and has a similar flavour. In shape and size it looks a bit like a rough-skinned swede (rutabaga), but the flesh is ivory coloured. It should be peeled thickly before using and immediately immersed in acidulated water to prevent it turning brown. Celeriac can be cubed and added to chutneys

BELOW: *Courgettes are best pickled when young and tender.*

instead of celery, or shredded and pickled with other root vegetables such as carrots. Dill and orange go especially well with celeriac.

RADISHES

These have a refreshing but very peppery flavour. The familiar small round or slightly elongated red or white varieties are sold all year round. The white Japanese radish, known as mooli or daikon, is larger and longer. This radish has a mild flavour and can be pickled.

HORSERADISH

This extremely pungent root is never eaten as a vegetable. The knobbly root is peeled and grated before being made into a condiment, usually with oil and vinegar. The astringency of its flavour makes horseradish the perfect accompaniment for rich or fatty foods.

KOHLRABI

The edible part of kohlrabi is the stalk or tuber. They are similar to turnips in size, appearance and taste. Use small kohlrabi for preserving because they toughen with age and their flesh becomes coarse and fibrous. Trim off the base and leaves, and peel thinly. Put them into acidulated water immediately to prevent browning. Use sliced or chopped in chutneys.

JERUSALEM ARTICHOKES

These small, knobbly tubers have a delicious nutty, sweet flavour when

cooked. Jerusalem artichokes can be used in chutneys and are delicious in spicy Indian relishes.

SQUASHES

These vegetables are large and have thick, tough, inedible skins. They also have fibrous flesh and large seeds. Different varieties of squash include butternut squashes, acorn squashes, spaghetti squashes and pumpkins. Their dense, sweet flesh cooks to a thick pulp and can be made into tasty jams. Winter squashes can also be used to add sweetness and a rich orange colour to chutneys.

MARROWS

These vegetables are known as large zucchini in the United States. Marrows have a pleasant, but bland, flavour and a high water content, so they are best brined before making into chutney.

CUCUMBERS

Due to their high water content, cucumbers are usually brined before preserving.

COURGETTES/ZUCCHINI

Picked when small, courgettes have a dark-green, shiny skin with light streaks, and creamy-coloured flesh. The seeds are very tender.

PATTY PAN SQUASHES

Shaped like flying saucers, patty pan squashes are green, yellow or striped. They look attractive cut into triangular wedges, then pickled.

ABOVE: *Firm red cabbage can be made into a delicious pickle with a fabulous dark-pink hue.*

CABBAGES

The many types of cabbage range from dark-green, crinkly-leaved Savoy to smooth, tightly wrapped white cabbages. From a preserving point of view, it is the firm white and red cabbages that are most suitable.

CAULIFLOWER

The creamy white florets of this mild-flavoured brassica feature in many savoury preserves, notably piccalilli, in which it is lightly cooked to retain its shape and crisp texture. It soaks up spices well and so is often used in hot and spicy Indian pickles and chutneys.

BROCCOLI

The long cooking required for chutneys would make broccoli disintegrate, so cut it into tiny florets and add towards the end of the cooking time in piccalilli and relishes.

ASPARAGUS

These can be included in luxurious preserves. Use when very fresh; asparagus stalks should be firm and the tips plump.

FENNEL

Florence fennel has squat, plump bulbs with a similar texture to celery, and green feathery fronds. It has an aniseed flavour that mellows when pickled. Chopped fennel can be added to chutneys, and the green fronds may be chopped and used in apple jelly.

CELERY

Crisp, crunchy celery may have white or green stalks, which should snap easily and not bend. Celery does not make a good pickle on its own, but is often added to mixed pickles, chutneys and relishes.

GLOBE ARTICHOKES

These look like enormous thistle-heads with purple-tinged green leaves. They are difficult to preserve whole, but the hearts can be pickled in a mild vinegar.

PEAS

Fresh peas in their pods have a delicate sweet flavour and make a tasty addition to chutneys and relishes. They should be added about 10 minutes before the end of cooking time, so that they stay firm and keep their colour.

BROAD/FAVA BEANS

These can be used in the same way as peas, but choose young fresh ones because the skins become tough as the beans mature.

GREEN BEANS

All types of green beans can be used to add flavour, colour and texture to preserves. French beans are small, narrow green beans with round pods that are available all year round; American green beans are similar, but much larger; flat runner beans are popular in Britain and are at their best when the home-grown crop is available in summer.

CORN

Corn cobs should be used as soon as possible after picking, before their natural sugars turn to starch. Baby corn cobs have a more delicate flavour than mature ones; they can be sliced into rounds and used in the same ways. Store corn cobs in the refrigerator for no more than a few days.

BELOW: *Corn kernels can be stripped from the cob and used to make a delicious relish.*

Herbs and spices

Flavourings are an essential part of most preserves and using the right amount is as important as choosing the right one. In some preserves only a subtle hint is needed; in others the flavouring is one of the main ingredients.

HERBS

Fresh and dried herbs are invaluable in savoury preserves. They can be added during the initial cooking, then removed, or finely chopped and stirred in towards the end of cooking. If dried herbs are used, then reduce the quantity by between a third to a half.

Tender herbs

Basil This highly aromatic herb bruises and discolours easily, so it can be steeped in vinegar until it imparts its flavour, then removed.
Chervil Use these tiny, soft and lacy leaves soon after picking. They have a flavour similar to parsley with a hint of aniseed, which goes well with mild, delicate vegetables.
Mint The many varieties of this herb add a fresh flavour to preserves, but should be used sparingly.
Parsley Curly and flat-leaf varieties are available. It is an essential herb in a bouquet garni.
Tarragon This herb is excellent for flavouring vinegars but is rarely used in its fresh form because it darkens and discolours on heating.

RIGHT: *Tender-leaved basil has a fragrant, peppery flavour that goes particularly well with tomato-based preserves.*

Robust herbs

Bay leaf Essential in bouquet garni, these dark-green glossy leaves should be dried before use.
Marjoram and oregano Popular in tomato preserves, these herbs should be added towards the end of cooking.
Rosemary Use this powerful fresh or dried herb in small quantities.
Sage A strong herb that often partners garlic and tomatoes.
Thyme This robust herb works well with preserves made from roasted vegetables and beans.

Aromatic and spicy herbs

Coriander/cilantro This adds a warm, spicy taste to Middle-Eastern, Asian and Indian chutneys and freshness to Mexican-style relishes.
Dill This herb has a subtle aniseed taste and dark-green, feathery leaves. It is good in mild relishes and pickles.

Fennel Part of the same family as dill, with a similar, but stronger flavour, it is good for flavouring vinegars.
Kaffir lime leaf This strong-tasting, aromatic leaf is used to flavour Thai and Malaysian preserves.
Lemon grass This is a tall hard grass, with a lemony aroma and taste. It is used in Thai preserves and should be bruised to release the flavour.
Lovage Similar to celery leaves with a peppery flavour, lovage is good with root vegetables and also in mixed vegetable chutneys.

Flowers

Many types of edible flowers and their leaves can be used to add fragrance and flavour to preserves.
Borage The tiny, brilliant blue or purple flowers of this plant can be crystallized or they can be used to decorate jellies.
Geranium leaves These give jams and jellies a subtle flavour.

Lavender Sprigs of fragrant lavender can flavour sugar, jams and jellies.
Rose Scented red, pink or yellow petals make wonderful jams and jellies. They are often combined with fruit juice, such as grape, and with added pectin, so that the preserve sets quickly without destroying the aroma of the petals. Be sure to use unsprayed roses.

SPICES

These can be hot, or warm and fragrant, and are used in all kinds of preserves for flavour and decoration.

Hot spices

Cayenne Made from ground dried chillies, cayenne is extremely hot and should be used sparingly.

Chillies Fresh chillies may be cooked in preserves to add heat, or added whole or chopped to clear pickles when bottling.

Chilli powder This hot spice is made from ground dried chillies.

Galangal This is related to ginger, with pink-tinged flesh. It is often used in Malasian- and Thai-style preserves.

ABOVE: *Fresh root ginger adds warmth and a lively, fresh, lemony flavour to all kinds of preserves.*

Ginger Root ginger may be used fresh, dried or ground. Preserved stem ginger can be added to conserves and marmalades.

Mustard There are three types of mustard seed: white, brown and black; black is the hottest. Whole mustard seeds are often included in pickles and ground mustard powder in relishes.

Paprika This rich, red spice is sold ground and used for its colour and flavour, which ranges from mild and sweet to strong and pungent.

Peppercorns Often added whole to pickles, these tiny round berries may be green, black or white.

Turmeric Although yellow turmeric has a distinctive warm, spicy taste, it is often used for its colour as an alternative to saffron.

Seed spices

Caraway seeds These mild, pungent seeds are in many northern European preserves, notably sauerkraut.

Cumin seeds Tiny light-brown seeds with a distinctive warm flavour, cumin is used in Indian, Mexican, North African and Middle-Eastern preserves.

Coriander seeds These small round seeds have a mild orange flavour and are usually included in pickling spice.

Dill seeds These small oval seeds taste like caraway, and are often used with cucumber pickles and relishes.

Fragrant spices

Allspice With an aroma and flavour like cloves, cinnamon and nutmeg, this is good used with orchard fruits.

Cassia and cinnamon The bark of evergreen trees, these are available ground or in sticks.

Cloves These tiny dried flower buds go well with apples and citrus fruit.

Juniper This gives gin its distinctive flavour; the berries are usually dried.

Nutmeg This has a warm nutty flavour. It is best bought whole and grated fresh.

ABOVE: *Golden saffron threads can be used to impart a subtle flavour and glorious colour.*

Mace This is the orange-coloured lacy outer covering of the nutmeg; it is sold as blades.

Saffron Made from dried stigmas of the *Crocus sativus*, this is the most expensive spice. It produces a golden colour and a bitter-sweet flavour.

Star anise This star-shaped, aniseed-flavoured spice looks wonderful in pickles and bottled preserves.

Tamarind This dark-brown pulp from the tamarind tree pod adds a unique sour flavour to preserves and pickles.

Vanilla Used to flavour bottled fruits, long, dark-brown vanilla pods (beans) have a sweet, warm, aromatic flavour.

Pickling spices

Various blends of pickling spices are available and include allspice, bay leaf, cardamom, coriander and mustard seeds, cinnamon, dried chillies, cloves, ginger and peppercorns.

Preserving ingredients

A few special ingredients are essential when making preserves, because they contribute to the keeping quality of the final jam, jelly or pickle. The four main preservatives are sugar, vinegar, salt and alcohol. These all help to prolong the life of the other ingredients used in the preserve by creating an environment in which micro-organisms such as moulds and bacteria cannot grow.

SUGAR

This is the key preservative used in jams, jellies, marmalades, curds and many preserved fruits. A high proportion of sugar is needed and if the sugar content is less than 60 per cent of the total weight of the preserve (for example, in low-sugar jams), this will affect the keeping quality of the preserve. These low-sugar jams and fruit preserves should be used within a few months or kept in the refrigerator to prevent the growth of mould.

Sugar also plays an important role in the setting of jams, jellies and marmalades. To achieve a good set, sugar should make up between 55 and 70 per cent of the total weight of the preserve. (High acid content in the fruit makes the exact amount of sugar less crucial.)

White sugars

These refined sugars produce clear, set, sweet preserves.

Preserving sugar has quite large, irregular crystals and is ideal for jams, jellies and marmalades. The large crystals allow water to percolate between them, which helps to prevent the preserve burning and reduces the need for stirring (which is important to avoid breaking up fruit too much). Use this sugar for the clearest preserves. If preserving sugar is unavailable, granulated sugar can be used instead.

Preserving sugar with pectin Also known as jam sugar, this sugar is used with low-pectin fruit. The sugar contains natural pectin and citric acid to help overcome setting problems. Preserves made with this sugar tend to have a shorter shelf-life and should be stored for no longer than six months.

Granulated sugar is slightly coarser than caster (superfine) sugar, less expensive and gives a clear result. Cube sugar is made from white granulated sugar that has been moistened, moulded into blocks, dried and cubed. It gives the same results as preserving sugar.

Brown sugars

These sugars give a pronounced flavour and darker colour to both sweet and savoury preserves.

Demerara/raw sugar is a pale golden sugar with a mild caramel flavour. Traditionally an unrefined sugar with a low molasses content, it may also be made from refined white sugar with molasses added.

Golden granulated sugar may be refined or unrefined. It can be used instead of white sugar for a hint of flavour and colour.

Soft brown sugar is moist, with fine grains and a rich flavour. It may be light or dark in colour and is usually made from refined white sugar with molasses added.

Muscovado/molasses sugar may be light or dark and is usually made from unrefined cane sugar. It has a deeper, more pronounced taste than soft brown sugar.

Palm sugar is made from the sap of palms and has a fragrant flavour. Sold pressed into blocks, it needs to be chopped before use. Light muscovado (brown) sugar is a good alternative.

Jaggery is a raw sugar from India with a distinctive taste. It must be chopped before use. Use a mixture of light brown muscovado and demerara sugar as an alternative.

BELOW: *White and golden sugars are a key ingredient used in sweet fruit preserves, jams and jellies.*

BELOW: *Raspberry and white wine vinegar are used both to preserve ingredients and to add a sharp, tangy flavour.*

VINEGARS

The word vinegar comes from the French *vin aigre*, meaning sour wine. Vinegar is made by exposing fruit or grain-based alcohol to air; a bacterial reaction then turns the alcohol into acetic acid and it is this acid that helps to prevent the growth of micro-organisms in pickles and preserves. Vinegar used for pickling must have an acetic acid content of at least 5 per cent.

Malt vinegar is made from a type of beer. It usually has an acetic acid content of 8 per cent, which allows it to be safely diluted by moisture and juices from fruit and vegetables. Malt vinegar usually contains caramel, which turns it a dark-brown colour. Its strong flavour makes it ideal for enlivening pickles, chutneys and bottled sauces. Pickling vinegar is simply malt vinegar that has been flavoured with spices.

Distilled malt vinegar has the same strong flavour as ordinary malt vinegar but is colourless and therefore suitable for making clear pickles and light preserves.

Wine vinegar may be red or white, depending on the original wine's colour. Most wine vinegars contain about 6 per cent acetic acid. White wine vinegar is mild and better for delicate preserves; red wine vinegar is slightly more robust and good for spiced fruits. Raspberry vinegar, made by steeping the fruit in wine vinegar, is excellent for pickled fruits.

Balsamic vinegar has a smooth, mellow flavour. Its low acidity makes it unsuitable for use on its own, but it can be used to flavour mild preserves, stirred in at the end of cooking.

Sherry vinegar is slightly sweet with a fairly strong flavour.

Cider vinegar has a slightly sharp taste and a fruity flavour. It is excellent for fruit preserves.

Rice vinegar Colourless, mild rice vinegar is made from rice wine and is often used for pickling ginger.

SALT

This is used as a seasoning, and in "brining", which draws out moisture from vegetables such as cucumber and marrow, making them crisp and preventing dilution of the preserve, which would reduce its keeping quality. Ordinary table and cooking salt is fine for this, but use pure crystal salt (kosher salt), or preserving or rock salt for clear pickles because ordinary table and cooking salts contain anti-caking ingredients that cause clouding.

ALCOHOL

Spirits, such as brandy and rum, and liqueurs, which are at least 40% ABV (alcohol by volume), can be used in preserving. Wine, fortified wine, and beer and cider have a lower alcohol content and therefore are not effective alone. These forms of alcohol should be either heat treated or combined with sugar to make them more suitable for use in preserving.

ACIDS

These help to set jams and jellies and prevent discoloration.

Lemon juice This adds pectin, prevents fruits from turning brown and enhances both the flavour and the colour of preserves. You can use lemon juice either freshly squeezed or bottled.

Citric acid is sold as fine white crystals and can be used instead of lemon juice in preserves.

Tamarind is a spice used both for its acid flavour and its character.

BELOW: *Many different kinds of salt – from coarse sea salt to preserving salt – can be used for pickling.*

Equipment

While very few specialist items are essential for preserving, having the correct equipment for the job will make the whole process easier and helps to ensure success. You will probably have most of the basic items, such as a large heavy pan, weighing scales or calibrated measuring cups, wooden spoons, a chopping board and a few sharp knives. However, a few specific items, such as a jam funnel for potting preserves and a jelly bag for straining fruit juices, will prove invaluable.

PRESERVING PAN

A preserving pan or large, heavy pan is essential. It must be of a sufficient size to allow rapid boiling without bubbling over (a capacity of about 9 litres/16 pints/8 quarts is ideal), wide enough for rapid evaporation of liquid so that setting point is reached quickly, and have a thick heavy base to protect the preserve from burning. A non-corrosive pan, such as one made of stainless-steel, is best for making preserves, especially pickles, chutneys and relishes with a high acid concentration. Traditional copper preserving pans, usually very wide at the top and sloping to a narrow base, are intended only for jam- and jelly-making and are unsuitable for preserves containing vinegar or lemon juice, or for acidic or red fruit.

SUGAR THERMOMETER

Invaluable for identifying the exact temperature for a perfect set. Choose one that goes up to at least 110°C/230°F, with a clip or a handle that can be attached to the pan, so that it does not slip into the boiling preserve.

JELLY BAGS

These are used to strain fruit juices from cooked fruit pulp for jelly-making. They are made from calico, cotton flannel or nylon. Some bags have their own stands; others have loops with which to suspend the bag.

MUSLIN/CHEESECLOTH

Used for making spice and herb bags; good for tying together pips and peel, particularly when making marmalade.

JARS AND BOTTLES

Clear glass is ideal for preserves because it is non-corrosive, you can easily check for trapped air bubbles when potting, and it looks pretty when filled. You can also use ordinary jam jars and bottles.

Specialist preserving jars are also available. These are designed to be heated to a high temperature. Non-corrosive seals are essential, particularly when potting acidic preserves and pickles.

PRESERVE COVERS

The cheapest way to cover jams, jellies and marmalades is to use a waxed paper disc and cellophane cover, secured by an elastic band; these covers are available to fit 450g/1lb and 900g/2lb jars.

FUNNELS

These make potting preserves considerably easier. A jam funnel with a wide tube (10–13cm/4–5in diameter) that fits into the top of the jar or container can make quick, clean work of filling jars.

An ordinary funnel with a slimmer tube is useful for adding liquid to jars of pickles or fruit as well as for bottling smooth sauces and jellies. Choose funnels made of heat-proof plastic or stainless-steel.

ABOVE: *A jelly bag with its own stand can make an easy job of straining jellies.*

ABOVE: *A jam funnel is a real time-saver when potting jellies, jams and conserves.*

HYDROMETER

This measures the density of sugar syrup and is used when bottling fruit and making jams and jellies.

SALOMETER

This is used to measure the amount of salt dissolved in brine for pickling.

BOWLS

Use non-corrosive bowls in different sizes for salting, soaking and mixing.

CHOPPING BOARDS

Plastic chopping boards are more hygienic than wooden ones because they are easier to clean properly. However, a wooden board is ideal to stand jars on when they are cooling.

SIEVES (STRAINERS) AND COLANDERS

Use nylon, plastic or stainless-steel sieves and colanders when straining acidic fruit or preserves.

WOODEN SPOONS

Long-handled spoons keep your hands at a safe distance from hot preserves.

SLOTTED SPOONS AND SKIMMERS

These are useful for lifting and draining solid ingredients and packing them into jars. A fine-mesh skimmer may be used for skimming jams and jellies to keep them clear.

VEGETABLE PEELERS

There are a number of different types of vegetable peeler available. Some peelers have a bean slicer attachment on the handle.

CORERS

When pickling or preserving whole fruits such as pears and apples, a corer can be used to cut out and remove the cores neatly without damaging the rest of the fruit.

STONERS/PITTERS

It can be fiddly to pit small fruits such as cherries with a knife, and almost impossible to keep the fruits whole while you are doing it. There are different types of pitters available for different sized fruits.

ZESTERS

The cutting edge of a zester has five little holes. When these are pulled firmly across the fruit, they remove fine strands of citrus rind, leaving the white pith behind.

CANELLE KNIVES

These have a v-shaped tooth that pares 5mm/$\frac{1}{4}$in strips of peel from fruit and vegetables, leaving grooves and creating a striped effect. If the fruit is then cut into slices, these will have attractively notched edges.

MANDOLINS

Firm fruits and vegetables, such as apples, beetroot (beet) and turnips, can be sliced or shredded finely and evenly using a mandolin. Most mandolins have adjustable cutting blades and supporting struts that hold the mandolin at the desired angle. Choose one with a safety guard to hold the food being sliced because the blades are extremely sharp and it would otherwise be very easy to cut yourself while slicing.

MINCERS AND FOOD MILLS

Both hand and electric mincers can save a good deal of time and energy when processing large quantities of fruit or vegetables.

GRINDERS

The traditional mortar and pestle is perfect for coarsely grinding small quantities of spices. For larger amounts or when a fine powder is required, use a spice mill or coffee grinder kept solely for that purpose.

ABOVE: *A cherry pitter effortlessly removes the pits from fiddly fruit.*

ABOVE: *A canelle knife and zester are ideal for paring off thin strips of citrus rind.*

Potting and covering preserves

Make sure you have enough jars and bottles, and the correct sterilizing equipment, before you start. Preparing, covering and storing preserves correctly helps to ensure they retain their colour, flavour and texture.

CHOOSING CONTAINERS

Always pot preserves in the right type of container. Pickles made from whole or large pieces of fruit or vegetables should be packed into large jars or bottles with a wide neck.

Smooth, pourable sauces or relishes can be stored in narrow-necked bottles, but thicker, spoonable preserves should be packed in jars.

STERILIZING

It is essential to sterilize jars and bottles to destroy any micro-organisms. An unsterilized jar or bottle may contain contamination that could cause the preserve to deteriorate or become inedible.

Check jars and bottles for cracks or damage, then wash thoroughly in hot, soapy water, rinse well and turn upside-down to drain. Jars and bottles may be sterilized in five different ways: by heating in a low oven, immersing in boiling water, heating in a microwave, hot-washing in a dishwasher, or using sterilizing tablets.

ABOVE: *Medium, wide-necked jars with plastic-coated screw-top lids are ideal for most preserves.*

Oven method

Stand the containers slightly apart on a baking sheet lined with kitchen paper. Rest any lids on top. Place in a cold oven, then heat to 110°C/225°F/ Gas ¼ and bake for 30 minutes. Cool slightly before filling. (If they are not used immediately, cover with a clean cloth and warm again before use.)

Boiling water method

Place the containers, open ends up, in a deep pan wide enough to hold them in one layer. Pour over enough hot water to cover them. Bring the water to the boil and boil for 10 minutes. Leave them in the pan until the water stops bubbling, then remove and drain

upside-down on a clean dish towel. Turn them upright and leave to air-dry for a few minutes. Immerse lids, seals and corks in simmering water for 20 seconds. (Only ever use corks once.)

Microwave method

This is useful when sterilizing only a few jars. Half-fill the clean jars or bottles with water and heat on full power until the water has boiled for at least 1 minute. Remove from the microwave. Swirl the water inside them, then pour it away. Drain and dry.

Dishwasher method

This is the simplest way to clean and sterilize a large number of containers at the same time. Put all the containers and lids in a dishwasher and run it on its hottest setting.

Sterilizing tablet method

This method is not suitable for delicately flavoured preserves because the tablets may leave a slight taste. Following the instructions on the packet, dissolve the tablets and soak the containers in the sterilizing solution. Drain and dry before use.

Storage times

Most preserves will keep for a year if packed and stored properly. Once opened, they should be eaten within 3 months. Some preserves have a shorter shelf life.

Fruit curds, butters and cheeses These can be stored in the refrigerator for 2–3 months and, once opened, they should be used within 4 weeks.

Relishes with a low proportion of vinegar and sugar and a short cooking time can be stored for up to 4 months. Once opened, store in the refrigerator and use within 4 weeks.

Low-sugar jams and specialist preserves rely on sterilizing for their keeping qualities and are usually processed commercially.

FILLING BOTTLES AND JARS

Most preserves should be potted into hot containers as soon as they are ready, particularly jellies and fruit preserves with a high pectin content. Whole fruit jams, marmalades with peel, and jellies with added ingredients, such as fresh herbs, should be left to cool for 10 minutes until a thin skin forms on the surface.

Some preserves, such as fruits bottled in alcohol or vegetables preserved in vinegar, are potted when cold rather than hot. The ingredients may be cooked, or simply washed, then packed into jars and cold alcohol or vinegar poured over them.

FILLING AND SEALING BOTTLES

Stopper bottles with a sterilized cork and dip in wax to seal them. Bottles are perfect for sauces and pourable relishes

1 Using a funnel, fill the hot sterilized bottles to within 2.5cm/1in of the top. Wipe the bottle rim clean.

2 Soak the corks in very hot water for 3–4 minutes, then push into the bottle tops as far as possible. Gently tap the corks in to within 5mm/¼in of the top of the bottle. Leave until cold.

3 To seal, tap down the corks as far as possible. Dip the top of each bottle in melted candle or sealing wax to coat. Leave to set, then dip a second time.

SEALING JARS

Cover jams, conserves, jellies, marmalades and fruit cheeses with a waxed paper disc, then cover the jar with cellophane held in place with an elastic band, or seal it with a screw top lid. Seal bottled fruits and pickled vegetables in jars with new rubber seals and vacuum or clamp-top lids. Seal chutneys and pickles with vinegar-proof lids.

JARS FOR BOTTLED FRUIT

When bottling fruit, the jars are heat-treated. There are several ways to do this. The filled jars may be heated in hot water, in the oven, or in a pressure cooker. As the fruit cools, a vacuum is created. Use jars specifically designed for heat treatment. Heat-treated preserves may be kept for up to 2 years.

The water bath method is suitable for fruits bottled in hot or cold syrup.

1 Wrap folded newspaper or cloth around each filled container, then stand on a metal trivet or thick layer of paper or cloth in a large heavy pan.

2 Pour tepid water around the jars, right up to the neck, then cover the pan with a lid.

3 Bring the water slowly to the boil (this should take about 25–30 minutes) then simmer for the required time.

4 Turn off the heat and ladle out some of the water. Using tongs or oven gloves, lift out the containers and place on a wooden board. If they have screw-band lids, tighten quickly.

5 Cool for 24 hours, then remove the screw bands or clips. Holding the rim of the lid, lift the container. If a jar is not sealed properly, it should be stored in the refrigerator and used quickly.

Heating times for water bath method

The following times are for fruit packed in hot syrup after boiling. Allow 5 minutes more for fruit packed in cold syrup.

Fruit	Minutes
Soft berries and redcurrants	2
Blackcurrants, gooseberries, rhubarb, cherries, apricots and plums	10
Peaches and nectarines	20
Figs and pears	35

Making jams, jellies and marmalades

These are made from fruit boiled with sugar until setting point is reached. They rely on pectin, sugar and acid for a good set. Pectin is a natural, gum-like substance, which is found in the cores, pips (seeds) and skins of fruits, and reacts with sugar and acid to form the gel that helps to set jams, jellies and marmalades.

TESTING PECTIN CONTENT

It is best to test for pectin content at an early stage in jam-making, and add extra pectin if necessary.

1 Cook the fruit until soft, then spoon 5ml/1 tsp of the juices into a glass. Add 15ml/1 tbsp methylated spirits (denatured alcohol) and shake.

2 After 1 minute a clot should form: one large clot indicates high pectin content; two or three small clots indicate pectin content is medium and should achieve a set; very small clots, or no clots at all, indicate low pectin content.

3 If the pectin content is medium, add 15ml/1 tbsp lemon juice for every 450g/1lb fruit. If it is low, add 75–90ml/5–6 tbsp pectin stock for every 450g/1lb fruit. Alternatively, add pectin powder or liquid, or use sugar containing pectin.

MAKING PECTIN STOCK

Home-made pectin stock is very easy to make and can be stirred into low-pectin fruit jams and jellies to improve their set.

1 Roughly chop 900g/2lb cooking apples, including the cores, peel and pips. Place in a large heavy pan and pour over enough cold water to cover. Bring the mixture to the boil, then reduce the heat, cover the pan and simmer for 40 minutes, or until the apple mixture is very soft.

2 Pour the mixture into a sterilized jelly bag suspended over a bowl. Leave to drain for at least 2 hours.

3 Pour the drained juices into the cleaned pan and boil for about 20 minutes, or until the volume is reduced by one-third.

4 Pour the pectin stock into 150ml/ $^1/_4$ pint/$^2/_3$ cup sterilized containers and store in the refrigerator for up to 1 week or freeze for up to 4 months.

5 To use frozen pectin stock, defrost it at room temperature, or overnight in the refrigerator, then stir it into the preserve.

Testing for a set

Some preserves reach setting point quickly, so check them early on.

Wrinkle test Remove the preserve from the heat and spoon a little on to a chilled plate. Leave to cool for 1 minute, then push the preserve with a finger; the top should wrinkle. If it wrinkles only slightly, return the preserve to the heat and cook for a further 2 minutes, then test again.

Flake test Coat a spoon in preserve; cool for a few seconds, then hold horizontally. When shaken, the jam should run off the side in one flat flake. Thermometer test Dip a jam thermometer into very hot water, then place in the preserve (do not touch the pan base). Marmalades and jams reach setting point at 105°C/ 220°F; jellies and conserves a degree lower.

MAKING JAM

Usually made with whole or cut fruit, jam should have a distinct flavour, bright colour and soft set.

Summer fruit jam

Use sound, slightly under-ripe fruit; over-ripe fruit contains less pectin and will not set well.

MAKES ABOUT 1.6KG/3½LB

900g/2lb mixed fruits, such as cherries, raspberries, strawberries, gooseberries, blackcurrants and redcurrants
2.5–20ml/½–4 tsp lemon juice
900g/2lb/4½ cups preserving or granulated (white) sugar

1 Weigh each type of fruit. Rinse and drain cherries, gooseberries, blackcurrants and redcurrants; wash raspberries and strawberries only if necessary; remove any stems and leaves and cut off any damaged parts.

2 Put the lemon juice in a large heavy pan: strawberries and cherries are low in pectin, so add 10ml/2 tsp lemon juice for each 450g/1lb fruit; add 2.5ml/½ tsp for each 450g/1lb raspberries; add no lemon juice for high-pectin fruits such as gooseberries and currants.

3 Put the prepared gooseberries, blackcurrants and redcurrants in the pan, then pour over 60ml/4 tbsp water and cook the fruit slowly over a low heat for 5 minutes until the skins have softened.

4 Add the cherries, raspberries and strawberries to the pan. (If using only these fruits, do not add any water.) Cook for 10 minutes until all the fruit is just tender.

5 Using the back of a spoon, crush one-third of the fruit to release the pectin. If using a lot of strawberries or cherries, do a pectin test at this stage of the recipe.

6 Add the preserving or granulated sugar to the pan and stir over a low heat until the sugar has dissolved completely.

7 Increase the heat and bring the mixture to the boil. Continue to boil rapidly for about 10 minutes, stirring occasionally, until setting point is reached (105°C/220°F). Skim off any froth that rises to the surface.

8 Remove the pan from the heat and leave to stand for 5 minutes. If necessary, skim off any froth from the surface of the jam, then stir to distribute any larger pieces of fruit. Pot, seal and label.

Is it a jam, conserve or spread?

Understanding the labels on store-bought preserves can be difficult. Here is a brief guide:

Jam This contains at least 30g/1¼oz fruit and 60g/2¼oz/generous ¼ cup sugar per 100g/3½oz jam. It may contain colourings and preservatives as well as gelling agents.

Extra jam At least 45g/1¾oz whole fruit per 100g/3½oz jam and no colourings, preservatives or flavourings.

Reduced-sugar jam This has a minimum of 35g/1½oz fruit and 30–55g/1¼–2¼oz sugar per 100g/3½oz jam.

Conserve This implies a quality jam with a high fruit content, but you should always check the label. Usually, the fruit is whole and steeped in sugar before cooking, giving a softer set.

Fruit spreads These are made from fruit pulps that have been sweetened with fruit juice.

MAKING SEEDLESS JAM FROM BERRIES

Some fruits, notably raspberries and blackberries, contain a large number of pips (seeds), which result in a very "pippy" jam or conserve. If you prefer a smooth jam without pips, they can be removed after initial cooking by pressing the fruit through a nylon or stainless-steel sieve (strainer).

MAKES ABOUT 750G/1²/³LB

450g/1lb/2²/³ cups raspberries
about 450g/1lb/2¹/₄ cups preserving
    or granulated (white) sugar

1 Use a mixture of just-ripe and a few slightly underripe berries to ensure a good set. Put the fruit in a large heavy pan and gently crush with the back of a wooden spoon to release the juices. Gently heat the fruit to boiling point, then simmer for about 10 minutes, stirring now and then, until the fruit is really soft.

2 Tip the fruit into a fine nylon or stainless-steel sieve placed over a large bowl and then push through the fruit purée using the back of the wooden spoon. Remove and discard the pips that are left behind in the sieve.

3 Measure the fruit pulp into the cleaned pan. Add 450g/1lb/2¹/₄ cups sugar for each 600ml/1 pint/2¹/₂ cups purée. Heat gently, stirring, until the sugar dissolves. Boil rapidly to setting point (105°C/220°F).

4 Skim any froth from the surface of the jam, then pot, cover and seal.

MAKING CHERRY JAM WITH COMMERCIAL PECTIN

Fruits with a low pectin content require additional pectin to achieve a good set. Adding commercial pectin is an easy way to do this. Jams made in this way need only a short boiling time, little or no water and a smaller proportion of fruit to sugar.

MAKES ABOUT 1.8KG/4LB

1.2kg/2¹/₂lb/6 cups pitted cherries
150ml/¹/₄ pint/²/₃ cup water
45ml/3 tbsp lemon juice
1.3kg/3lb/generous 6³/₄ cups sugar
250ml/8fl oz/1 cup liquid pectin

1 Put the cherries, water and lemon juice in a large pan. Cover and cook for 15 minutes, stirring, until the cherries are tender.

2 Add the sugar to the fruit mixture and stir over a low heat until all the sugar has dissolved completely. Bring to the boil and boil rapidly for 1 minute.

3 Pour the liquid pectin into the pan and stir it into the jam. Return the mixture to the boil and cook for a further 1 minute.

4 Remove the pan from the heat and, using a slotted spoon, skim off any froth from the surface.

5 Set the jam aside and then leave it to stand for 5 minutes.

6 Stir the jam briefly to distribute the fruit evenly, then pot and seal.

Pectin content of fruit

Although the pectin content of fruits can vary depending on variety, growing conditions and when the fruits were picked, the list below can be used as a good basic guide to the set that will be achieved.

High Apples, blackcurrants, cranberries, damsons, gooseberries, grapefruit, lemons, limes, loganberries, redcurrants, quinces.

Medium Apricots (fresh), apples (eating), bilberries, blackberries (early), grapes, mulberries, peaches, plums, raspberries.

Low Bananas, blackberries (late), cherries, elderberries, figs, guavas, japonicas, melons, nectarines, pears, pineapples, rhubarb, strawberries.

MAKING CONSERVES

Conserves are similar to jams, but have a slightly softer set and contain whole or large pieces of fruit. The fruit is mixed with sugar and sometimes a little liquid, then allowed to stand for several hours or even days. The sugar draws out the juices from the fruit, making it firmer and minimizing the cooking time needed. The fruit should be just ripe and even in size. Not all fruit is suitable for making conserves; tough fruit skins do not soften when sugar is added, so some fruits, such as gooseberries, are no good for making conserves.

Strawberry conserve

This strawberry conserve takes several days to make, so make sure you allow plenty of time for preparing and chilling at each stage.

MAKES ABOUT 1.3KG/3LB

**1.3kg/3lb small or medium
    strawberries, hulled**
1.3kg/3lb/generous 6³/4 cups sugar

1 Layer the hulled strawberries in a large glass bowl with the sugar. Cover with clear film (plastic wrap) and chill for 24 hours.

2 Transfer the mixture to a large heavy pan. Heat gently, stirring occasionally, until the sugar has dissolved. Bring to the boil and cook steadily (not rapidly) for 5 minutes. Cool, then place in a bowl, cover with clear film and chill for 2 days.

3 Pour the mixture into a large pan, bring to the boil and cook steadily for 10 minutes. Remove from the heat. Set aside for 10 minutes. Stir, ladle into warmed sterilized jars and seal.

FLAVOURING CONSERVES

Conserves are more luxurious than jams and often include dried fruit, nuts, and spirits or liqueurs. These extra ingredients should be added after setting point is reached.

   When adding dried fruit or nuts, chop them evenly and allow about 50g/2oz/¹/₂ cup fruit or nuts per 750g/1²/₃lb conserve.

   Choose spirits or liqueurs that complement the fruit's flavour. For example, add apricot brandy or amaretto liqueur to apricot conserve, kirsch to cherry conserve, and ginger wine to melon conserve; allow 30ml/2 tbsp for every 750g/1²/₃lb conserve.

Top tips for successful jam-making

• Always use the freshest fruit possible and avoid over-ripe fruit.

• If you wash the fruit, dry it well and use promptly because it will deteriorate on standing.

• Cook the fruit very slowly at first over a low heat to extract the maximum amount of juice and pectin. Stir the fruit frequently until very tender, but do not overcook. (Remember that fruit skins toughen once sugar is added.)

• Warm the sugar in a low oven for about 10 minutes before adding it to the fruit. This will help the sugar to dissolve.

• Stir the preserve to ensure the sugar is completely dissolved before boiling.

• Do not stir the mixture frequently when boiling. This lowers the temperature and delays reaching setting point.

• It is wasteful to remove scum too often. To help prevent scum from forming, add a small amount of unsalted (sweet) butter (about 15g/¹/₂oz/1 tbsp for every 450g/1lb fruit) when you add the sugar.

• Do not move freshly potted preserves until they are cool and have set completely.

MAKING JELLIES

Jellies are made using juice strained from simmered fruit, which is then boiled with sugar to setting point. There is little preparation, other than rinsing fruit, and roughly chopping larger fruit, but you do need plenty of time to make the jelly itself. The secret to a beautifully clear jelly lies in straining the fruit pulp through a jelly bag, drip by drip, for several hours.

The basic principles of jelly-making are the same as those for jam and the same three substances – pectin, sugar and acid – are needed for the jelly to set. A perfectly set jelly should retain its shape and quiver when spooned out of the jar. Fruits that are low in pectin, such as strawberries, cherries and pears are not suitable on their own for making jellies, so are usually combined with high-pectin fruit.

Since the fruit pulp is discarded in jelly-making, the yield is not as large as in jam-making. For this reason many jelly recipes have evolved to make the most of wild fruits, which are free, or gluts of home-grown fruit.

YIELD OF JELLY

The final yield of jelly depends on how juicy the fruit is. In view of this, the juice, rather than the fruit, is measured and the amount of sugar is calculated accordingly. As a general rule, 450g/ 1lb/2¼ cups sugar is added for each 600ml/1 pint/2½ cups juice. (If the fruit is very rich in pectin, the recipe may suggest adding slightly less sugar.) As a rough guide, recipes containing 450g/1lb/2¼ cups sugar will make about 675–800g/1½–1¾lb jelly.

Redcurrant jelly

MAKES ABOUT 1.3KG/3LB

1.3kg/3lb just-ripe redcurrants
600ml/1 pint/2½ cups water
about 900g/2lb/4½ cups preserving
**   or granulated (white) sugar**

1 Check the fruit is clean. If necessary, rinse in cold water and use a little less water in the recipe. Remove the stalks.

2 Place the fruit in a large heavy pan with the water and simmer for about 30 minutes, or until the fruit is very soft and pulpy. Stir occasionally.

3 Put the fruit in a sterilized jelly bag suspended over a large bowl. Drain for 4 hours, or until it stops dripping.

4 Discard the pulp remaining in the bag. Pour the juice into the cleaned pan and add 450g/1lb/2¼ cups warmed sugar for each 600ml/ 1 pint/2½ cups of juice.

5 Heat the mixture gently, stirring frequently, until the sugar has completely dissolved, then increase the heat and bring to the boil. Boil rapidly for about 10 minutes, or until setting point is reached.

6 Remove from the heat, then skim any froth from the surface of the jelly. Pot the jelly immediately because it will start to set fairly quickly. Cover and seal the jelly while it is still hot, then leave to cool completely. Label and store in a cool, dark place.

FLAVOURING SAVOURY JELLY

Savoury jellies are often flavoured with fresh herbs such as thyme, mint, sage and rosemary.

1 To add flavour, simply add sprigs of herbs at the beginning of cooking. Woody herbs should be removed before draining because stems may damage the jelly bag.

2 When adding chopped herbs to the finished jelly, even distribution can be difficult. If it is too hot, pieces may float to the top. To overcome this problem, put the herbs in a sieve (strainer) and sprinkle with a little water to dampen them.

3 Leave the jelly to stand until it just starts to form a thin skin on top, then stir in the chopped herbs. Pot straight away in very warm, but not hot, sterilized jars. Seal, then cool before labelling.

USING A JELLY BAG

Jelly bags, which are made from heavy-duty calico, cotton flannel or close-weave nylon, allow only the juice from the fruit to flow through, leaving the skins, pulp and pips (seeds) inside the bag. The fruit pulp and juices are heavy, so strong tape or loops are positioned on the corners for hanging the bag securely on a stand, upturned stool or chair.

1 Before use, sterilize the jelly bag by scalding in boiling water. This also helps the juices run through the bag, rather than being absorbed into it.

2 If you don't have a jelly bag, you can use three or four layers of sterilized muslin (cheesecloth) or a piece of fine linen cloth instead. Simply line a large nylon or stainless-steel sieve with the muslin or linen.

3 Carefully suspend the jelly bag or lined sieve over a large bowl to catch the juice. Make sure the bag or sieve is secure before spooning some of the simmered fruit and juices into it. (Don't add too much to start with.) Allow the fruit to drain for a while, then add some more fruit.

4 Continue gradually adding fruit in this way until it has all been placed in the bag or sieve, then leave to drain until it stops dripping completely. Some fruits will take 2–3 hours to release all their juice, while others may take as long as 12 hours.

5 Immediately after use, wash the jelly bag thoroughly, then rinse several times to remove all traces of detergent. Ensure the bag is completely dry before storing. It may be reused many times, but sterilize it before every use.

Top tips for successful jelly-making

• There is no need to peel or stone (pit) fruit before cooking because all the debris will be removed during straining. However, it is important to discard bruised or mouldy parts. Rinse the fruit only if dusty or dirty.

• If you are using fruits that require longer cooking, such as apples, chop the fruit very finely to reduce the cooking time required. Cooking the fruit for a shorter time also helps to give the jelly an intense, fresh flavour.

• Simmer fruit very gently to extract pectin and avoid excess evaporation. When cooking hard fruits, cover for the first half of cooking to reduce the amount of liquid lost.

• You can cook some fruits, such as currants, in the oven to make jellies. Place in an ovenproof dish with 75ml/ 5 tbsp water, cover and cook at 140°C/275°F/Gas 1 for 50 minutes, stirring occasionally, until pulpy. Drain through a jelly bag. Add 425g/15oz/ generous 2 cups sugar for every 600ml/1 pint/2½ cups strained juice.

• Jellies set very quickly, so pot immediately. Warm a stainless-steel funnel in the oven, or rinse a plastic one under hot water and dry it, then use to pot the jelly. If the jelly starts to set in the pan, warm it briefly until liquid again.

• As you fill the jars with jelly, gently tap them to remove air bubbles.

• Although you can add a little butter to jam to disperse any scum, do not do this with jelly – the butter will make it cloudy.

MAKING MARMALADE

This preserve consists of a jelly base, usually with small pieces of fruit suspended in it. The name marmalade is derived from the Portuguese word *marmelo*, meaning quince, and it was from this fruit that marmalades were first made.

Modern marmalades are usually made from citrus fruits, or citrus fruits combined with other fruits such as pineapple, or flavoured with aromatic spices. They can range from thick and dark to light and translucent.

The citrus peel is shredded and cooked with the fruit juices and water until soft and tender, then boiled with sugar to make the marmalade. Citrus peel requires long, slow cooking in a large amount of water to become soft. The pith of Seville (Temple) oranges, lemons and grapefruits becomes clear when cooked, but that of sweet oranges does not, so the pith should be scraped off the rind before shredding and cooking.

As well as classic marmalade, there is also jelly marmalade. This is a perfect jelly for people who enjoy the flavour of marmalade but do not like the peel that is suspended in the jelly. Rather than adding the shredded rind to the juices and water in the pan, the rind is tied in a muslin (cheesecloth) bag to keep it separate. The juices are then strained and boiled to setting point. The jelly may be left plain and potted as it is, or a little of the shredded rind can be stirred into the jelly just before potting. As with any jelly, it is difficult to give an exact yield for jelly marmalade.

Seville orange marmalade

Bitter Seville oranges are very popular for marmalade-making.

MAKES ABOUT 2.5KG/5¹/₂LB

900g/2lb Seville (Temple) oranges, washed
1 large lemon, washed
2.4 litres/4 pints/10 cups water
1.8kg/4lb/generous 9 cups preserving
    or granulated (white) sugar

1 Wash and dry the fruits. If you are using waxed fruits, scrub the skins gently. Halve the fruits and squeeze out the juice and pips (seeds), then pour into a muslin- (cheesecloth-) lined sieve (strainer) set over a bowl.

2 Remove some of the pith from the Seville orange and lemon peels and reserve, then cut the remaining citrus peel into narrow strips.

3 Add the reserved pith to the pips in the muslin and tie together to make a loose bag. Allow plenty of room so that the water can bubble through the bag and extract the pectin from the pith and pips.

4 Place the shredded peel, juices and the muslin bag in a large preserving pan and pour in the water. Using a clean ruler, measure the depth of the contents in the preserving pan and make a note of it.

5 Slowly bring the mixture to the boil and simmer for 1¹/₂–2 hours, or until the peel is very soft and the contents have reduced by about half their depth.

6 To check the peel is cooked, remove a piece from the pan and cool for a few minutes. Press it between finger and thumb; it should feel very soft.

7 Using a slotted spoon, carefully remove the muslin bag from the pan and set aside until cool.

8 When the bag has cooled sufficiently, squeeze as much liquid as possible from it back into the pan to extract the maximum amount of pectin from the pips and pith.

9 Add the sugar to the pan and stir over a low heat until the sugar has completely dissolved.

10 Bring the marmalade to the boil, then boil the mixture rapidly for about 10 minutes until setting point is reached (105°C/220°F). You may also use the flake or wrinkle test to check the set.

11 Using a slotted spoon, remove any scum that may have formed on the surface of the marmalade.

12 Remove the pan from the heat, then leave the marmalade to cool until a thin skin starts to form.

13 Leave the marmalade to stand for about 5 minutes more, then stir the mixture gently in order to distribute the peel evenly.

14 Carefully ladle into hot sterilized jars, then cover and seal them tightly. Label when cold.

RIGHT: *Limes are equally delicious made into sweet marmalades and salty pickles.*

Top tips for successful marmalade-making

• Wash citrus fruits well. Most fruits have a wax coating to help prolong their shelf life. This should be removed before making the marmalade. Alternatively, buy unwaxed fruit, but always rinse before use.

• Shred peel slightly thinner than required because the rind will swell slightly during cooking.

• Coarse-cut peel will take longer to soften than finely shredded peel. To reduce cooking time, soak the peel for a few hours in the water and juices before cooking.

• If the fruit needs to be peeled, put it in a bowl of boiling water and leave to stand for 2 minutes. This will help to loosen the skins, and make peeling easier. The rind's flavour will leach into the water, so replace some of the water with the soaking water.

• If using small, thin-skinned fruits such as limes, cut them into quarters lengthways. Slice the flesh and rind into thin or thick shreds. If using larger, thick-skinned fruits such as grapefruits, pare the peel, including some white pith, and shred. Cut the fruit into quarters, remove the remaining pith and roughly chop the flesh.

• To make a coarse-cut preserve, boil the whole fruit for 2 hours until soft, then pierce with a skewer to test. Use a slotted spoon to lift out the fruit, halve, prise out the pips, then tie them loosely in muslin (cheesecloth) and add to the hot water. Boil for 10 minutes, then remove the bag. Slice the fruit and return to the pan. Stir in the sugar until dissolved, then boil to setting point.

• Shredded peel should be simmered gently; fierce cooking can make it tough. Check that the peel is soft before adding sugar; it will not soften further after you have added it.

• For easy removal, tie the muslin bag of pith and pips with string and attach it to the pan handle. It can then be lifted out of the boiling mixture easily.

• If the fruit contains a lot of pith, put only a small amount in the muslin bag with the pips. Put the remaining pith in a small pan, cover with water and boil for 10 minutes. Strain the liquid and use in place of some of the measured water for the recipe.

• To flavour marmalade with liqueur or spirits, add 15–30ml/1–2 tbsp for every 450g/1lb/2¼ cups sugar. You can stir it in just before potting. Unsweetened apple juice or dry (hard) cider may be used to replace up to half the water to add flavour to marmalades made with sharper fruits such as kumquats.

Fruit butters, curds and cheeses

These rich, creamy preserves were once the highlight of an English afternoon tea during Edwardian and Victorian times. Fruit curds and butters are delicious spread on slices of fresh bread and butter, or used as mouthwatering fillings for cakes. Fruit cheeses and butters are also very good served with roast meat, game or cheese.

Fruit curds are made from fruit juice or purée cooked with eggs and butter. They are always made in a double boiler or a bowl set over a pan of simmering water to prevent the eggs from curdling. Whole eggs are generally used, but if there is a lot of juice, egg yolks or a combination of whole eggs and yolks give a thicker result. Fruit curds have a soft texture and short keeping qualities.

Fruit butters and cheeses are made from fruit purée boiled with sugar, useful if you have a glut of fruit because they require a relatively high proportion of fruit.

Fruit butters are lower in sugar and cooked for a shorter time than cheeses, producing a soft, fruity preserve with a short shelf life.

Fruit cheeses have a very firm texture and may be set in moulds and turned out to serve.

MAKING FRUIT BUTTERS

Smoother and a lot thicker than jam, fruit butters have a spreadable quality which is not unlike that of dairy butter. Many recipes for fruit butter also contain a small amount of butter in them.

Apricot butter

MAKES ABOUT 1.3KG/3LB

1.3kg/3lb fresh ripe apricots
1 large orange
about 450ml/³/₄ pint/scant 2 cups water
about 675g/1¹/₂lb/scant 3¹/₂ cups caster (superfine) sugar
15g/¹/₂oz/1 tbsp butter (optional)

1 Rinse the apricots well under cold running water, then cut them in half and stone (pit) them. Roughly chop the flesh.

2 Carefully remove the apricot skins with a knife, then discard, unless you are going to puree the fruit by pressing through a sieve (strainer).

3 Scrub the orange well. Then using a sharp knife, thinly pare off 2–3 large strips of rind, avoiding any pith. Squeeze out the juice from the orange and reserve in a small bowl.

4 Put the apricots, and the orange rind and juice into a large heavy pan. Pour over enough water to cover the fruit. Bring to the boil, half-cover the pan, then simmer for 45 minutes.

5 Remove the orange rind from the pan, then blend the apricot mixture in a food processor until it is very smooth. Alternatively, press the mixture through a fine nylon or stainless-steel sieve.

6 Measure the apricot purée, return it to the cleaned pan and add 375g/13oz/1³/₄ cups of caster sugar for each 600ml/1 pint/2¹/₂ cups of fruit purée.

7 Heat the mixture gently, stirring, until the sugar has dissolved completely. Bring to the boil and then boil for 20 minutes, stirring frequently, until thick and creamy.

8 Remove the pan from the heat. If using, stir in the butter until it has completely melted. (The butter gives a glossy finish.) Spoon into warmed sterilized jars and cover. Store the butter in the refrigerator and use within 6 months.

MAKING FRUIT CURDS

Fruit curds are usually made with juice from citrus fruits, or other acidic fruits, such as passion fruits.

Lime curd

MAKES ABOUT 675G/1½LB

5 large, ripe, juicy limes
115g/4oz/½ cup butter, cubed,
**   at room temperature**
350g/12oz/scant 1¾ cups caster
**   (superfine) sugar**
4 eggs, at room temperature

1 Finely grate the lime rind, being careful not to include any of the bitter white pith. Halve the limes and squeeze out the juice. Place the rind in a heatproof bowl set over a pan of just simmering water, then strain in the juice to remove any fruit or pips (seeds).

2 Add the butter and the sugar to the bowl. Heat gently, stirring, until the butter melts; the mixture should be barely warm, not hot. Beat the eggs with a fork, then strain through a fine sieve (strainer) into the warm mixture.

3 Keeping the water in the pan at a gentle simmer, stir the mixture continuously until the curd is thick enough to coat the back of a wooden spoon. Do not overcook as the curd will thicken further as it cools down.

4 Spoon into warmed sterilized jars, then cover and seal when cool. Store in a cool, dark place, ideally in the refrigerator. Use within 2 months.

MAKING FRUIT CHEESES

These sweet, firm preserves are known as cheeses because they are stiff enough to be cut into slices or wedges rather like their dairy counterparts. This name is particularly appropriate when the cheeses are set in moulds and turned out. They may be made either from fresh fruit, or from the pulp left from making jellies.

Cranberry and apple cheese

MAKES ABOUT 900G/2LB

450g/1lb/4 cups fresh cranberries
225g/8oz cooking apples
600ml/1 pint/2½ cups water
10ml/2 tsp lemon juice
about 450g/1lb/2¼ cups sugar
glycerine, for greasing (optional)

1 Rinse the cranberries under cold running water and place them in a large heavy pan.

2 Wash the apples thoroughly and cut them into small pieces (there is no need to peel or core them). Add the water and lemon juice to the pan.

3 Cover the pan with a lid and bring the mixture to the boil; do not lift the lid until the cranberries stop popping because they often jump out of the pan and can be very hot.

4 Simmer the fruit mixture gently for about 1 hour, or until the fruit is soft and pulpy.

5 Press the mixture through a fine nylon sieve into a bowl.

6 Weigh the purée, then return it to the cleaned pan, adding 450g/1lb/2¼ cups sugar for every 450g/1lb purée. Gently heat, stirring, until the sugar has dissolved completely.

7 Increase the heat and simmer gently until it is thick enough that a spoon leaves a clean line through the mixture when drawn across the pan. This may take as long as 30 minutes. Stir frequently to prevent burning.

8 Spoon into warmed sterilized jars and seal, or into moulds or jars greased with glycerine and cover with clear film (plastic wrap) when cool. In sealed jars it will keep for 1 year; in covered moulds, refrigerate until required. Eat within 1 month.

Pickles

These can be sharp or sweet or a combination of the two. They are made by preserving raw or lightly cooked fruit or vegetables in spiced vinegar. They may be eaten alone or as a condiment with cheese or cold meat.

TYPES OF PICKLES

There are two types of pickles: clear or sweet. To make clear pickles such as pickled onions, salt or brine is used to extract water from the vegetables, giving them a crisp texture, before they are bottled in vinegar. To make sweet pickles, fruit or vegetables are usually cooked until tender, then bottled in a sweet vinegar syrup.

Fruit and vegetables used for pickling should be firm and young. Small varieties such as baby (pearl) onions, beetroot (beets), and gherkins which can be pickled whole, are particularly good. Large vegetables, such as

BELOW: *Shallots can be pickled whole.*

cucumbers, marrows (large zucchini), cabbage and cauliflower should be sliced or chopped.

Most pickles have to be matured in a cool, dark place for a minimum of 3 weeks for at least 2 months to develop and mellow their flavour before eating. Pickled cabbage loses its crisp texture so should be eaten within 2 months of making.

Take care when packing fruit or vegetables into jars – they should not be packed too tightly because the vinegar must surround each piece. It is important to fill jars to the brim and avoid trapping any air. This will cause discoloration and may encourage the growth of bacteria and moulds.

Large, wide-necked jars are ideal for pickling. Screw-top jars with lids that have plastic-coated linings such as those used for commercial pickles are a good choice. Vinegar reacts with metal, causing it to corrode and flavour the pickle, so always avoid metal tops when pickling.

CLEAR PICKLES

For clear pickles, the ingredients are usually soaked in brine. This draws out the vegetables' moisture, making them more receptive to vinegar and preventing the juices from diluting the vinegar. Pure or kosher salt should always be used because iodized salt will taint the pickle with an iodine flavour and the additives in table salt will make it cloudy. There are two types of brine: dry brine, where the salt is sprinkled over the vegetables; and wet brine, where the salt is dissolved in water first.

MAKING SPICED PICKLING VINEGAR

Ready-spiced pickling vinegar, and jars or packets of mixed pickling spices, are readily available from many supermarkets. However, you can make your own, adapting the combination of spices according to personal preference and the ingredients that are to be preserved. You can use any variety of vinegar, but make sure that it has an acetic acid content of at least 5 per cent.

Basic spiced pickling vinegar

MAKES 1.2 LITRES/2 PINTS/5 CUPS

15ml/1 tbsp allspice berries
15ml/1 tbsp cloves
5cm/2in piece fresh root ginger, peeled and sliced
1 cinnamon stick
12 whole black peppercorns
1.2 litres/2 pints/5 cups vinegar

1 Put all the spices in a jar and pour over the vinegar. Cover the jar and leave to steep for 1–2 months, shaking occasionally. After this time, strain the vinegar and return it to the cleaned jar. Store it in a cool, dark place until ready to use.

COOK'S TIP

To make quick pickling vinegar for immediate use, put all the ingredients in a pan and heat gently to boiling point. Simmer for about 1 minute, then remove from the heat, cover and leave to infuse (steep) for 1 hour. Strain and use.

PICKLING GREEN VEGETABLES

The colour of green vegetables tends to be lost if stored for more than a few months, although their flavour remains the same. Blanching them in boiling water mixed with 5ml/1 tsp bicarbonate of soda (baking soda) for 30 seconds helps retain their colour, but destroys the vitamin C content.

SWEET PICKLES

For these pickles, fruit and some vegetables such as cucumbers are preserved in sweetened vinegar. They are excellent served as an accompaniment to cold meats, poultry and cheeses. Pickled apples or pears are also delicious served with hot baked ham or grilled (broiled) meat such as lamb chops.

Sweet pickles are made with distilled malt, wine or cider vinegar rather than brown malt vinegar, which would overpower the flavour and affect the colour of the fruit.

To offset the sharpness of the vinegar, a fairly large amount of sugar is added, usually between 350g/12oz/scant 1¾ cups and 450g/1lb/2¼ cups to every 300ml/½ pint/1¼ cups vinegar.

ABOVE: *Mild-tasting cucumbers are perfect for pickles and relishes.*

Unlike vegetables, fruits do not need to be brined before pickling. Fruits that are pickled whole, such as plums and cherries, should be pricked before the initial cooking in order to allow the vinegar syrup to penetrate the skin and stop the fruit shrivelling. Some fruits, such as berries, become very soft when pickled and are therefore better preserved in sugar syrup or alcohol.

Spices and flavourings add zest to sweet pickles. They are best infused in the vinegar at the start of cooking, but also look attractive added to the bottle when packing the preserve. Use whole spices such as cinnamon, cloves, allspice, ginger, nutmeg and mace; ground spices will make the pickle murky. Citrus rind and vanilla pods (beans) also add a wonderful taste and aroma. Robustly flavoured herbs, such as rosemary and bay leaves, work well in sweet pickles.

PICKLING DRIED FRUITS

All sorts of dried fruits can be made into excellent pickles. The fruits soak up the pickling syrup, becoming soft, succulent and juicy. Dried apricots, peaches, pears, figs, prunes and mango slices are perfect for pickling.

Dried fruit pickles do not need as much sugar as pickles made with fresh fruit; dried fruits are already packed with sugar. A small amount of liquid, such as apple juice or water, may be used to rehydrate the fruit before pickling. This prevents the fruit soaking up too much vinegar and the flavour becoming overpowering. When

ABOVE: *Whole cinnamon sticks are often used to flavour sweet pickles.*

pickling light-coloured dried fruits, such as apricots, pears or apples, use light-coloured sugars and vinegars. Dark-coloured fruits, such as figs and prunes, can be pickled using malt or red wine vinegar, and darker sugars.

Raspberry vinegar

Fruit vinegars are perfect for making sweet pickles and are very easy to make at home.

To make about 750ml/1¼ pints/ 3 cups raspberry vinegar, put 450g/1lb/generous 2½ cups fresh raspberries in a bowl with 600ml/ 1 pint/2½ cups white wine or cider vinegar. Cover the bowl with a cloth and then leave it in a cool place for 4–5 days, stirring each day. Strain the vinegar through a nylon or stainless-steel sieve (strainer) and discard the raspberries. Pour the liquid into a jelly bag suspended over a large non-metallic bowl or jug (pitcher). Leave to drain, then pour the vinegar into sterilized bottles and seal. Store in a cool, dark place and use within 1 year.

Chutneys, relishes and sauces

Chutneys are made from finely cut ingredients, cooked slowly with vinegar, a sweetener and frequently spices or other flavourings to make a thick, savoury, jam-like mixture. Relishes are similar, but they are cooked for a shorter length of time to give a crisper, fresher result. Sauces are made with similar ingredients to chutneys, but have a thinner consistency and are sieved to make a smooth purée.

MAKING CHUTNEYS

Onions and apples are often included in chutneys, but almost any fruits and vegetables can be used. Chutneys should be matured in a cool dark place for at least 2 months before eating.

BELOW: *Apples are used in almost every type of preserve – from sweet jellies to spicy relishes.*

Tomato chutney

MAKES ABOUT 2.25KG/5LB

50g/2oz whole pickling spices, such as
    peppercorns, allspice berries, dried
    chillies, dried ginger and celery seeds
450g/1lb onions, chopped
900ml/1½ pints/3¾ cups malt vinegar
1kg/2¼lb ripe tomatoes, skinned
    and chopped
450g/1lb cooking apples, peeled, cored
    and chopped
350g/12oz/1½ cups soft light brown sugar
10ml/2 tsp salt
225g/8oz/1 cup sultanas (golden raisins)

1 Tie the spices together in a muslin (cheesecloth) bag and put in a large, heavy pan with the onions and vinegar. Bring slowly to the boil, then simmer for 30 minutes until the onions are tender.

2 Add the tomatoes and apples to the pan and simmer for about 10 minutes.

3 When the apples and tomatoes are softened and start to break down slightly, add the sugar and salt to the pan.

4 Stir the mixture over a low heat until the sugar has completely dissolved, then stir in the sultanas.

5 Gently simmer the chutney for 1½–2 hours, stirring occasionally to prevent the mixture sticking. The chutney is ready when it is thick and no liquid is on the surface. Draw a wooden spoon across the base of the pan: it should leave a clear line in the mixture.

6 Remove the pan from the heat and cool for 5 minutes. Discard the spice bag. Stir the mixture to ensure the chutney is evenly mixed, then spoon into warmed sterilized jars.

7 Use the handle of a wooden spoon to release any trapped air bubbles and ensure that the chutney is packed down well.

8 Seal the jars then leave to cool. Store in a cool, dark place. Leave to mature for at least 1 month before eating. Use within 2 years.

RELISHES

Fruits and vegetables in relishes are cut into slightly smaller, neater pieces, and wine vinegar or cider vinegar is more frequently used than malt vinegar. Relishes contain a low proportion of vinegar and sugar, so do not keep for long. They can be eaten immediately, or chilled and used within 2–3 months.

RELISHES WITH THICKENED SAUCES

Some relish sauces are thickened with flour or cornflour (cornstarch). Mustard or turmeric may be added to give a yellow colour, such as in corn relish, piccalilli and chow-chow. The vegetables should retain their shape and be slightly crunchy, not soft.

MAKING SAUCES

Those sauces made with vegetables low in acid must either be stored in the refrigerator and consumed quickly, or heat-treated.

Tomato ketchup

MAKES ABOUT 600ML/1 PINT/ 2 ¹/₂ CUPS

900g/2lb ripe tomatoes
225g/8oz shallots, peeled
2cm/³/₄ in piece fresh root ginger, peeled
2 garlic cloves, peeled
150ml/¹/₄ pint /²/₃ cup cider vinegar
about 40g/1¹/₂oz/scant ¹/₄ cup granulated (white) or soft light brown sugar
5ml/1 tsp paprika
5ml/1 tsp salt

1 Chop the tomatoes, shallots, ginger and garlic fairly small, so the mixture cooks quickly and keeps its fresh flavour.

2 Put all the chopped vegetables together in a large heavy pan. Slowly bring to the boil, stirring frequently until the juices start to run. Reduce the heat, cover and simmer for 20 minutes, stirring frequently, until the shallots are tender.

3 Spoon the tomato mixture into a sieve (strainer) placed over a clean pan and press through using the back of a spoon. Alternatively, push the mixture through a food mill.

4 Bring to the boil, then reduce the heat and simmer for 45 minutes, or until reduced by half.

5 Add the vinegar, sugar, paprika and salt and stir to combine. Simmer for a further 45 minutes, stirring frequently, until well reduced and thickened.

6 Remove the pan from the heat. Pour the hot sauce into hot sterilized bottles, then seal with corks and heat-treat.

7 Store in a cool, dark place, preferably the refrigerator. If it has been heat-treated, the sauce will keep for up to 2 years; if it has simply been bottled, it will keep for up to 2 months in the refrigerator.

Top tips for successful chutney-making

• Use malt vinegar for its intense flavour. Wine vinegar or cider vinegar are better for preserving colourful or light-coloured vegetables because they will not spoil their colour.

• Brown sugar gives the richest flavour and colour; demerara (raw) sugar and golden granulated sugar give a caramel flavour; white sugar retains the colour of light ingredients.

• Never cover the pan when making chutney. Cooking it uncovered allows the liquid to evaporate and the chutney to thicken. Towards the end, stir frequently to prevent it catching and burning on the base of the pan.

• Always store chutney in a cool, dark place: warmth causes it to ferment, and bright sunlight affects the colour.

BELOW: *Chutneys and relishes are delicious and ideal spread in sandwiches.*

Bottled fruits and **fruits preserved** in alcohol

Bottling is a traditional method of preserving fruit in syrup, while fruits preserved in alcohol make luxurious instant desserts, served with crème fraîche or ice cream. One of the best-known fruit and alcohol preserves is German rumtopf, which means rum pot.

BOTTLING FRUITS

Although superseded by freezing, bottling is more suitable for some fruits, such as peaches, pears, grapes and oranges; the method is less suitable for preserving soft berries such as raspberries.

PRESERVING FRUITS IN ALCOHOL

Pure alcohol is the best preservative because bacteria and moulds are unable to grow in it. Clear liqueurs, such as eau de vie, orange liqueur, kirsch and amaretto, or spirits such as brandy, rum and vodka, which are at least 40% ABV, may be used.

When using alcohol to preserve, it is usually best to combine it with sugar syrup because high-alcohol liqueurs and spirits tend to shrink the fruit. Most fruits are first simmered in syrup, which helps to tenderize the fruit and kills the bad enzymes.

Poached pears

Fruit is often poached in syrup until just tender before bottling.

MAKES ABOUT 1.8KG/4LB

225g/8oz/scant 1¼ cups sugar
1.2 litres/2 pints/5 cups water
1 orange
1 cinnamon stick
2kg/4½lb cooking pears

1 Put the sugar and water in a pan with a thin strip of orange rind and the cinnamon. Heat gently until the sugar has dissolved, then bring to the boil and simmer for 1 minute.

2 Squeeze the juice from the orange, and strain. Peel and core the pears, then toss in orange juice as each one is prepared.

3 Add the pears to the syrup in a single layer. Place baking parchment over the pears to keep them immersed. Poach the pears for 15 minutes until they are tender and slightly translucent; the syrup should hardly bubble so that the fruit holds its shape.

4 When cooked, remove from the heat, bottle and heat-treat.

Nectarines in brandy syrup

For extra flvour, add vanilla or cinnamon to the syrup.

MAKES ABOUT 900G/2LB

350g/12oz/1¾ cups preserving
    or granulated (white) sugar
150ml/¼ pint/⅔ cup water
450g/1lb firm, ripe nectarines, halved and
    stoned (pitted)
2 bay leaves
150ml/¼ pint/⅔ cup brandy

1 Put the sugar and water in a pan and heat gently, stirring until dissolved. Bring to the boil, then reduce heat and simmer for 10 minutes. Add the nectarines, reduce the heat until barely simmering and poach the fruit until almost tender. Add the bay leaves 1 minute before the end of cooking.

2 Turn off the heat and stand for 5 minutes. Lift out the fruit and pack into hot sterilized jars. Bring the syrup to the boil and cook for 3 minutes.

3 Leave to cool slightly, then stir in the brandy. Pour the syrup into the jars over the fruit. Tap the jars to release any air and seal. Store in a cool, dark place and use within 1 year.

Dried fruits and **vegetables**

Removing moisture from foods is one of the oldest methods of preserving. Traditional techniques depend on the correct proportions of sunlight, heat and humidity for successful results. If food is dried too fast, moisture can get trapped and spoil it; if it is dried too quickly, micro-organisms may start to grow.

Most commercially dried fruits and vegetables, such as apricots, figs and tomatoes, which are high both in sugar and acid, are still wind- and sun-dried in the way they have been for centuries.

To re-create these conditions, an airy place with a steady temperature is needed. A very warm room or cupboard may be used if the temperature is constant, but the most efficient way is to use an oven on the lowest setting.

A fan oven is ideal for drying fruits and vegetables because of the constant circulation of air provided by the fan. If you are using a conventional oven without a fan, leave the door open with the tiniest possible gap, or open the oven door frequently during the drying process in order to let the steam escape. Be careful to ensure that the temperature does not become too high, or the fruit or vegetables will

cook and shrivel. If necessary, turn off the oven occasionally and leave it to cool down.

Choose firm, fresh and ripe fruit and vegetables for drying. Citrus fruits and melons consist mainly of water, so do not dry well, nor do berry fruits because they discolour and become very seedy. To help preserve the dried fruit and prevent discoloration, the prepared pieces should be dipped into a very weak brine solution, or acidulated water, before drying.

Dried apple rings

15ml/1 tbsp salt, or 90ml/6 tbsp lemon juice, or 30ml/2 tbsp ascorbic acid (vitamin C) powder
1.2 litres/2 pints/5 cups water
900g/2lb firm, ripe apples

1 Put the salt, lemon juice or ascorbic acid powder in a large bowl and pour in the water. Stir gently until completely dissolved.

2 Peel and core the apples, then cut into rings slightly thicker than 5mm/¼in. As soon as each apple has been cut, put the rings into the bowl of water to prevent discoloration.

3 Leave the apple rings in the bowl of water for at least 1 minute before lifting out carefully with a slotted spoon. Pat the rings dry with kitchen paper.

4 Thread the apple rings on to wooden skewers, leaving a small space between each ring.

5 Carefully rest the skewers on the oven shelves, allowing the apple rings to hang between the gaps. Leave the door slightly ajar. Dry the apples at 110°C/225°F/ Gas ¼ for about 5 hours, or until the apple rings resemble soft, pliable leather.

6 Remove the apple rings from the oven and leave to cool. Very crisp fruits and vegetables should be stored in airtight containers, but leathery, pliable fruits are better stored in paper bags or cardboard boxes; storing in plastic bags may make them go mouldy.

7 To reconstitute the dried apple slices, put in a bowl and pour over boiling water. Leave to soak for at least 5 minutes, then place in a pan and cook in the soaking liquid.

Index